DBT: Dialectical Behaviour Therapy

Regain Your Healthy and Happy Life with Mindfullness and Positivity and Wiping Out the Harmful Depression, Anxiety, and Panic in This Essential Guide of Dialectical Behaviour Therapy.

BY

Tom Bhowey

DBT: Dialectical Behaviour Therapy

Break Free from The Chains of Depression, Anxiety, Trauma, Mindlessness and Initiate a Healthy Start with This Practical Guide of Mindfulness, Positive Emotions, and Happiness.

BY

Tom Bhowey

Table of Contents

DBT: Dialectical Behaviour Therapy

An Ultimate Practical Therapy Guide to Getting Rid of Anger, Panic, Anxiety, and Negativity and Replacing it with Lifetime Happiness in This Workbook of Deep Wisdom.

BY

Tom Bhowey

Table of Contents

Introduction

If you've ever come across profuse emotions, you know very well what's being talked here. Sometimes, a day comes, and you feel like you hit by a storm. In those moments, a sufferer feels understandably terrifying to feel things because he/she does not want to get swept away by their emotions. The problem is, the more you try to hide or put a stop to it, the more profuse they get. It's necessary to keep in mind that attempting to hide or stop feelings doesn't work.

Dialectical Behavioral Therapy was introduced to the world by Marsha Linehan in 1993. It's an outpatient treatment founded on cognitive-behavioral principles for the patients of parasuicidal behavior in women with Borderline Personality Disorder (BPD). Marsha defines parasuicidal behavior as "any intentional, self-harming behavior with or without suicidal aim, including suicidal attempt and self-damaging behaviors. BPD is a chronic disorder that includes signs such as identity disturbance, unstable relationships, feelings of emptiness, stress, or self-mutilating behaviors.

Dialectical Behaviour Therapy is strongly effective at helping and assisting people in managing profuse emotions. It is supported by research that dialectical behavior therapy makes a person strong at coping distress without losing self-control or behaving in a rubbish manne Many people are suffering from overwhelming emotions generation by generation. It feels like a button is turned to full volume on much of how they feel. When they get annoyed, dizzy, or frightened, it showcases like a strong wave that may sweep them off their feet.

A fair amount of researches advocates that the probability of developing overwhelming emotions may be hardwired from birth. But it can also arise due to childhood neglect. A deeply disturbing or distressing experience during our development can make us vulnerable to depressing emotions. It's a fact that profuse emotions are often deep-rooted into our genetics, but that doesn't mean that its incurable or impossible to treat. This book will address how to control personality disorders, which very possibly be beneficial to you.

In this book, we will go through what is Dialectical Behavior therapy (DBT), how it works, history of DBT, DBT for substance abusers, personality disorders and taking control of personality disorders and much more which will be very beneficial at changing, altering or betterment of your life

Overview of DBT

Dialectical Behavior Therapy has its roots glued with cognition-based therapies. Its primary focus is to instill positive thoughts in a person's mind to live the moment and defend himself or herself against depression, anxiety with strength, strategies to alter severe emotions, which are causing problems in a person's life and effective interpersonal communication.

Brief History

DBT was introduced in the 1980s by Dr. Marsha Linehan and colleagues. They introduced different techniques and treatments to cope with and manage negative thinking patterns as well. DBT is a derivation from a philosophical process called dialectics. The word dialectics refers to the combination of two opposites. The core goal of DBT is to create a dynamic that promotes two opposed goals for individuals that are 'accept and change.' It is a state where two persons have different points of view about a specific subject, but they try to reach the truth through reasoned and logical arguments.

This conceptual framework evolved when a dilemma arose while developing the effective treatment of suicide patients.

Dialectics makes three assumptions:

- Change is inevitable.
- Everything is interconnected.
- Two different thoughts can be channeled in line to get to a closer approximation of the truth.

Validation was also offered by Linehan, which emphasizes that patients must listen with real care and concern. This verbal and non-verbal support gets maximum engagement from the patient, which helps in diagnosing and treating.

- Listening with empathy and real concern by showcasing engagement through verbal and non-verbal cues such as saying

  "ah-ha" and "what else."

- Evaluate and describe a person's unsaid emotions.

- Go through all what individual shared with accuracy.

- Showcase that you acknowledge the individual's current state in relation to prior history or syndrome he or she faced.

How DBT works?

Dialectical Behavioural Therapy process can happen in 3 types of settings:

- A class where a patient is treated through interactive sessions and assignments

- Individually by a professional trainer

- Phone coaching by a therapist

Every therapeutic technique has its own purposes, but certain key elements remain the same:

- **Support:** assisting in identifying pleasant qualities and exercising them.

- **Behavioral: a** detailed study of problematic behaviors by replacing them with sound and positively effective ones.
- **Cognition:** altering of behavior or actions which are not helpful.
- **Skill Set:** capability enhancement by learning the latest skills
- **Acceptance and change:** accepting of life, thoughts, and yourself and making changes where necessary
- **Collaboration:** effective communication and working as a team.

DBT Strategies

Sufferers of DBT are taught four strategies to alter their behavior effectively:

Mindfulness

It's a strategy that has a primary focus on "living in the moment." By doing that, a person can learn what's happening inside him/her through emotions, sensations, and feelings. Mindfulness also lets a person evaluate what's happening outside, such as what you touch, hear, touch, or see. It helps a person in mitigating negative thoughts and gives emotional strength to stay calm and composed.

Distress Tolerance

This strategy helps a person in accepting and instilling his or herself in line with the current situation. Specifically, a person learns four techniques: self-soothing, distraction, improving the movement and evaluation of pros and cons. This strategy will enable a person in advance to prepare himself against overwhelming emotions and cope with them in a positive and effective manner.

Interpersonal Effectiveness

This strategy, called Interpersonal Effectiveness, helps a person to become more confident in a relationship. It's a result of listening with attention and effective communication and giving respect to others and yourself too.

Emotional Regulation

This strategy equips a person with a skill-set that helps in strengthening and sound running of an emotional system. Emotional regulation gives specific knowledge about adjusting your emotions, including intensity, when you've it how you react to it. Emotional vulnerability can be minimized and replaced with positive emotional thoughts by identifying and tackling negative emotions such as anger.

What DBT treats?

While Dialectical Behavior Therapy provides a swift and efficient cure for human beings suffering from personality disorders (Paranoid, Anti-social, Avoidant, Borderline, etc.), it also works for numerous mental health conditions such as:

- Attention Deficit Hyper Disorder (ADHD)
- Binge Eating Disorder
- Bipolar Disorder
- Substance Use Disorder
- Anxiety Disorder

- Traumatic and Post Traumatic Disorder

- Depressive Disorders (chronic depression, major depressive disorders)

- Suicidal and Self-harming Behaviour

What is DBT?

Dialectical Behavior Therapy (DBT) is a branch associated with the tree of Cognitive Behavioural Therapy (CBT). CBT seeks to instill pleasant behavioral changes by recognizing and eradicating anxious thoughts. DBT is performed to cure personality disorders, including parasuicidal. A person learns to replace depressing behaviors by tackling or altering with pleasant thoughts. It is strengthened and advocated by many studies that DBT can be helpful in curing parasuicidal and drug abuse problems.

DBT Treatment Targets

Patients normally have different problems before getting treatment of dialectical behavior therapy. DBT exercises a set of targets that help the professional in making up the mind for choosing an order to cure the problem. In descending order, targets are:

- **Life-threatening behaviors:** Such behaviors that may lead to the life-ending of the patient are addressed on priority. Such behaviors include ideation of suicide, interaction about suicide and suicidal injury, etc.

- **Therapy-interfering behaviors:** Secondly, any behavior which may interfere in the process of a client receiving effective treatment. Such behaviors include late to a session, appointments abandoning, and showing a glimpse of uninterest towards treatment goals. They can be at the part of the patient or therapist.

- **Quality of life behaviors:** Thirdly, behaviors that are interrupting quality running of everyday life of the patient. For example, disorders, financial instability, a broken family, etc.

- **Skills acquisition:** Replacement of outdated, orthodox, and ineffective behaviors with new positive behaviors to help a patient in achieving his or her goals

DBT Treatment Stages

The process of Dialectical Behavioural Therapy is performed at four steps, which are classified in line with an individual's behavior and professionals get along with their client to edging closer to their primary mission of tailoring life in a positive manner by reaching goals of every stage.

- **At Stage 1,** the human being is in a sorry state of affairs, and their behavior uncontrolled. They may attempt to end their life, inflict injury, use drugs, and involve in other self-deteriorating behaviors. Usually, at the initial stage of DBT, a person states their situation as "rotting in hell." The Therapist tends to get a patient from the nexus of uncontrollability to a state of 'behavioral controllability.'

- **At Stage 2,** the patient is passing the everyday life of disparity, where the continuous hurt from poor validation and prior life traumas never ends. Their behaviors are controlled, but emotional experiences hinder them. The therapist tries to get the client out from a life of disparity to a life of aesthetic pleasure.

- **At Stage 3,** the patient is taught a set of life skills, which makes every day easier to live by defined life goals, self-respect, and seeking of internal happiness and calmness.

- **At Stage 4,** few people need this stage where they look forward to getting a deeper

  ⍰ meaning of life. The therapist moves a patient from a sense of alienation or unfulfillment to a life enriched with happiness, chortles, and liberty.

□

□

⍰ **DBT Cost Effectiveness**

□

⍰ There are certain researches with shreds of evidence that claim and advocate that DBT has reduced the expenses of treatment. A data shared has estimated that Dialectical Behaviour Therapy has cutoff treatment expenses by 56 percent compared to last year's figures. Massive decrease in hospital expenditures, which are 26000 dollars per client, clearly outweighed the convalescent services expense increase, which is 6500 dollars per client. A research conducted by Meyers and Colleagues in 2014 found that old-age dialectical behavioral therapy patients used 48 percent less convalescent mental health services in the following year. The most important find of study is, length of stay after DBT decreased by 69 percent and usage of highly costed inpatient services cut off by quite staggeringly 50 percent. Quite astonishingly, the study reported that those individuals who received DBT spent 6000 dollars less in the next year compared to the prior year before Dialectical behavior therapy. To sum up, the cost decreased close to a quarter of a million-dollar.

It is hard to compare other counties' cost-effective studies with the United States of America because of currency fluctuation, inflation, unstable exchange rate, and a greater difference in healthcare costs. However, a study completed in Australia found that hospital days were cut short by 70 percent after just six months of the Dialectical Behavioural Therapy program. King of similar results is also produced in Wales and Sweden.

An institute examined benefits rather than cost and found out that 38.05 dollars of economic gain are received over every 100 cents spent on the Dialectical Behavior Therapy program. Similarly, a study from England proposes a 1 percent depletion in self-destructiveness was attained overspending every 36 Great Britain Pound GBP. A German study concluded a 50 percent reduction in illness cost compared to the prior year. In short and comprehensive, financial evaluation of Dialectical Behavioural Therapy treatment indicates that: a) clear and staggering reduction in cost compared to the prior year; b) less costly than usual hospital treatment; c) economic benefit to the diagnosing and treatment institute; d) probability of decrease in over-all societal cost.

History of DBT

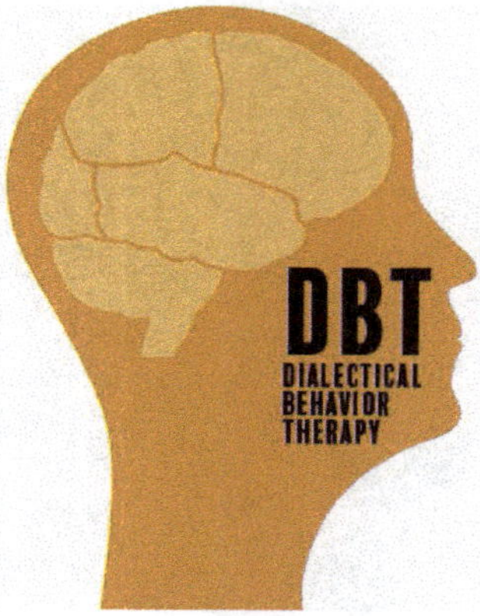

In the era of the 1970s and ’80s, therapists found really struggled in finding an effective cure for individuals who repeatedly shown parasuicidal behavior. The basic problem behind was an individual's low self-confidence or lack of positive thinking patterns. As a result, individuals were constantly attempting suicide. Since a lot of time was utilized to diagnose this situation, it left very little time to concentrate on the issues that could enact real change in the individual’s life. In such moments of difficulty, Dialectical Behavioral Therapy (DBT) was developed by Marsha Linehan in 1993 as a treatment for borderline personality disorders. She initially developed it to treat women only. But as time progressed, the application of Dialectical Behaviour Therapy was expanded to

other populations and disorders. When Marsha Linehan started working with clients of Borderline Personality Disorder (BPD), she initially followed an orthodox cognitive-behavioral approach. She started noticing that people with BPD had a strong, negative reaction to the heavy concentration on change. That is inherent in the cognitive-behavioral tradition of recognizing and tangling beliefs, with the purpose of changing distress behaviors. Linehan identified that people with BPD are really sensitive. They tend to react powerfully to circumstances in which they feel invalidated.
They are usually treated harshly in their childhood by caregivers. Such therapy created an environment in which kid's emotions were often invalidated.

Invalidation is a result of rejection, punishment, denial, or discrimination by the caregiver.

Linehan proposed that 'change emphasis' of orthodox CBT is profoundly invalidating for patients. This 'change emphasis' provokes a sense between these highly sensitive clients that there's something wrong about them. This situation recalled back distress-filled childhood memories of invalidation. They were not properly engaged nor benefitted from therapy because it felt painfully invalidating to them. Linehan proposed few innovations to her therapeutic approach in response to such a situation. A significant modification was made on the acceptance and validation of the patient's emotional and behavioral situations. People look for treatment because their life is not running smoothly. They ask for help to make some productive changes. This introduced a therapeutic quandary for Marsha because 'acceptance and change' are conflicting agendas. She thought of moving back and forth between change and acceptance during therapy in a dialectical manner as a solution to this dilemma.

The term dialectic means to seek a compromise between things that seem incompatible. Sometimes, she'd accepting and validating, and other times she'd be promoting and rooting change. She would switch according to her patient's ability to manage and tackle with emotions that surrounded requests for change.

The primary focus in Dialectical Behaviour Therapy is on reinforcement and integration of 'acceptance and change.' Instead of having one-dimensional conversations with the patient, she would engage him/her through the use of real-world examples to extract the desired responses. One by one, Linehan, the DBT developer, was able to teach her patients how to react with versatility in different situations. A key component is 'mindfulness,' which has roots in the practices of Buddhism. It emphasizes on staying present in the moment and experiencing what's happening inside and outside without judgment.

DBT Modules

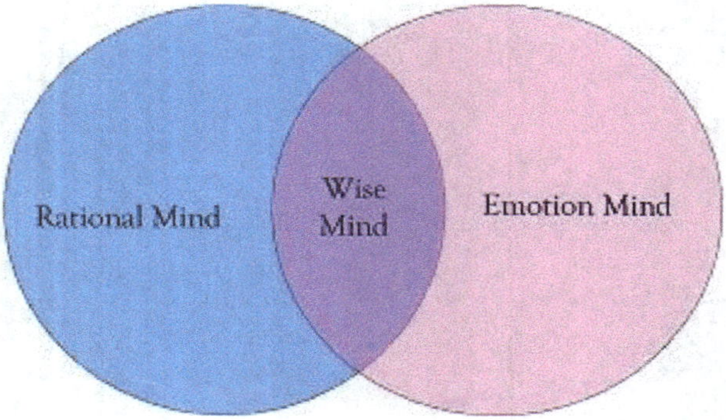

Dialectical behavior therapy consists of four modules known as mindfulness, distress tolerance, emotional regulation, and interpersonal effectiveness.

Module#1

Mindfulness

Mindfulness is a base on which every other skill set is delivered in dialectical behavioral treatment. It is from the core ideas behind the science of DBT. It is moment-to-moment awareness, without judgment, of one's thoughts, feelings, or body sensations. The basic idea of mindfulness is inspired and picked up from orthodox religious exercise, but it doesn't circle around any metaphysical sentiment concept. Dialectical Behaviour Therapy teaches to pay heed, staying in the moment, unjudgemental, experiencing a person's behavior and actions with perspective. The procedure of mindfulness helps to evaluate what's happening outside by making people aware through five senses: taste, touch, sound, sight, and smell. The process of mindfulness is heavily inclined and dependent upon 'acceptance.' It's a skill where the patient accepts the situation, attached meanings, and gelled emotions to it. Due to this, less distress prevails, which results in less and less discomfort.

Acceptance and Change

The initial stages of DBT introduce the person with the phenomenon of 'change & acceptance.' It's important that the patient shall feel comfortable with the idea of therapy because every other is dependant upon his positive will. Before emphasizing learning, one must understand radical learning, which means a person must face pleasant and disturbing situations without being judgy. Acceptance is interconnected with regularized emotions, which counts on the core foundation of thorough acceptance. Once a person starts catching the phenomenon of acceptance, the concept of change is never far. A DBT contains five states to change, which a therapist review according to the patient. They are pre-contemplation, contemplation, preparation, action, and maintenance in descending order. At the first stage, pre-contemplation, the patient does not know about their problem. In the second stage, contemplation, the patient identifies and realize illness. Third stage, preparation, patient steps forward to take precautionary measures which can be in the form of reaching a therapist or researching solution by self. At stage four called action, which is self-explanatory, the patient takes practical action and gets treatment. Lastly, at maintenance, the patient strengthens the concept of change to eradicate the chances of relapsing.

"What" Skills

What skills means the behavior, feelings, actions that a person exercises while practicing mindfulness, which includes observing, describe, and participate. "Observe" means to pay heed on purpose to the present moment. "Describe" means giving a dress of words to observation. "Participate" means getting involved in the present moment. There must be one activity performed at a single time.

Observe

A person must be nonjudgmental in experiencing inside and outside environment. This greatly helps in understanding what's happening in a specific moment. Dialectical behavior therapy advocates the idea of "Teflon mind," which means the strength and skill to let go of experiences and feelings without sticking them into mind.

Describe

It is about expressing nonjudgmentally what a person has observed during the time of "observation." After the observation of the inner or outer self with the five above mentioned senses, a person can easily give words to what he/she observed, which helps in a better understanding of the situation.

Participate

Total attention and involvement in the activity which is happening in the current moment

How" Skills

It's about how an individual observes, describes, or participate while exercising mindfulness without being judgmental. The person stays one-mindful with effectiveness. The difference in "what" skill and "how" skill is that, 'what' emphasis on which skill should be done at a time and 'how' shed light on the usage of all aforementioned skills at the same time.

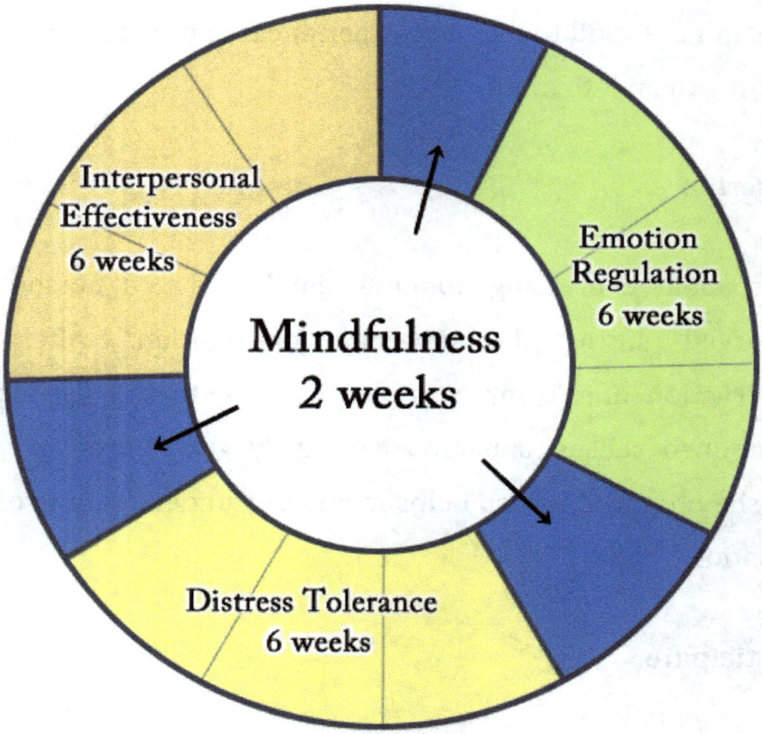

Nonjudgmentally

It's a stage where the person tells about the facts he/she discovered in the process of observing while staying pure of any bias or maladaptiveness. These are not a description of facts, rather words of judgments an individual made. A nonjudgmental view gets very fewer disagreements from others.

One-mindfully

One-mindfully means paying heed on one particular phenomenon. It helps in preventing getting out of that specific emotion, which leads to a lack of focus on the current moment.

Effectively

Exercising the skills which really work.

Module#2

Distress Tolerance

In today's world, the focus is shifting towards giving mental health treatment, which can be because of any depressing event, i.e., broken family, relationship problems, death, work issues, illness, terrorism, and many other types of traumatic events. This type of issue is generally tackled by individual-centered psychodynamic, psychoanalytic, and narrative treatments along with teachings from metaphysical as well as spiritual influencers. The emphasis of DBT is about learning and equipping oneself with skills of bearing and getting through moments of hardship skillfully. The main idea behind this therapy is to recognize negative behaviors, feelings, and actions, ways to cope with it,/to learn the skill-set to change it with a positive thinking pattern. The therapist teaches techniques of how not to become overwhelmed or hide behind the anxious situation.

DBT of emotional distress tolerance is treated by six different types of skills. Those skills are:

Skill 1

TIPP Skills

It's arguably the most growing and effective skill of distress tolerance. It vanishes the symptoms in a jiffy. Therapist nowadays encourages patients who are emotionally profuse and prone to inflict self-harm to use TIPP skill. TIPP stands for Temperature, intense exercise, paced breathing, and paired muscle relaxation.

- **T**ipping the temperature of the face with cool water. The ideology behind this is to bring on the dive reflex and physiology down to slow it down

- Usually, when we are in the state anger, our body feels hot, to counter this, splash your face with ice-cold water, or sit in a room with an on AC. Changing your temperature will burn off the heating body and cool you down on the emotional and physical level.

- Twenty minutes of exercise with full **i**ntensity

- Do as much intense exercise as much intense your emotions are. This can be in the form of a 50-meter sprint, planks, jumps, or any other exercise till you have fired all your cylinders. Scientifically proven, increasing the oxygen level diminishes stress levels.

- **P**aced breathing. Sometimes a thing as simple as managing your breath can effectively decrease emotional pain. There are different breathing techniques used, such as 'breathe it out' or 'box breathing' etc. but each one has a four seconds interval. Breathe in for four seconds, hold, breathe out, and hold for four seconds at every stage. Calm and steady breathing pattern diminishes a person's fight or responses.

- **P**aired muscle relaxation

- The Science behind paired muscle relaxation is really cool. When you tighten your muscles, relax it and give a few seconds to rest, the muscle will be more relaxed than it was before, and you will feel far more relaxed. Science advocates that relaxed muscle needs less oxygen, so your heart-rate and breathing level will come down.

Skill 2

Distract with ACCEPTS

Skill used to track away an individual from a series of distress emotions for the time being. The DBT distress tolerance acronym ACCEPT stands for activities, contributing, comparison, push away, thoughts, and sensations. These strategies are designed in a way to let an individual manage his or her emotions until the problem is solved.

- **A**ctivities --- usage of pleasant activities which an individual enjoys

- A person may keep himself busy in any activity such as reading a novel, calling your lover, making a banana shake, or ironing clothes. Any activity which keeps an individual busy and away from negative thinking pattern will help. If an individual finishes an activity, he/she must move on to another. And like this, one will be staying away from overwhelming emotions.

- **C**ontribute --- assisting and helping others or community in general and doing anything kind to help another individual. Services offering may relieve the negative thinking pattern in a couple of ways. While providing services, one may get his mind off the problems. Generally, we feel good after helping someone else, which may help a struggling individual in dealing with depression or stress. These acts can be in the form of taking a loved one for dinner, washing clothes of a friend, cleaning the house to help your wife, mother or cooking something for neighbors, these all acts of free service might help an individual to get off his/her mind from negativity.

- **C**omparisons --- comparison of one-self with others who are in a sorry state of affairs or when the individual was in a cocky situation

- It can be a rewind back of the individual's life when he was struggling with difficult challenges and profuse emotions or thinking about how he/she is blessed to have a home and food and while so many in the world are fighting and dying for a piece of bread and having no place to sleep. The idea behind is not to increase the pain of feelings but to pave a new avenue to what an individual is going through in the current mood.

- **E**motions --- try to feel differently by provoking your sense of humor. You have the strength to invoke completely different emotions of your present overwhelming feeling. If you're feeling depressed, try to take a walk around the park. If you're feeling anxious, try to see the pictures of puppies. In short, providing a dose of the different emotions helps in reducing the intensity of overwhelming emotions.

- **P**ush Away --- putting yourself at secondary positon and temporary letting something else take the primary concentration in your mind.

  It's very okay to push something aside when you cannot deal with it in a running moment. You can shift your focus towards some other activities, thoughts and can come back later to the disturbing issue.

- **T**houghts --- compelling your mind on thinking about something else

  - It's precisely about replacing negative, overwhelming thoughts with activities that simultaneously busy your mind. It roughly can be in the shape of saying alphabets or counting backwardly or solving a puzzle. This shift of focus will assist in avoiding personality-destructive behavior until you're in a position of getting emotional regulation.

  - **S**ensation --- perform something filled and enriched with intensity. Usage of five senses to self-soothe at the moments of distress can be helpful. A self-soothing behavior can be in the shape of taking a hot shower, calming music, eating your favorite snack, or watching an interesting movie. In plain terms, anything which may feel appealing to senses can significantly help at tackling the negative situation.

Skill 3

Self-soothing

A skill in which a person behaves in a gentle, nice, and comfortable manner to oneself. It's a way to enhance distress tolerance by using body senses. Self-soothing through senses diminishes the intensity of emotional pain very quickly. Above mentioned senses and their uses are:

- **Sight**

  Usage of vision to concentrate on something else. Start counting how many places you see, how

many colors are there in the room, or pull out your phone and start scrolling social media, photos, or anything.

- **Hearing**

Start paying focus on any sound you can hear, may it be bird's chirp or romantic music or your favorite song, turn the volume and shake your body with the vocals.

- **Taste**

A certain smell may be of food or fragrance or anything which gives you pleasure and distracts you from the negative emotions.

- **Touch**

You can embrace your sense of touch by running fingers through your hair, grabbing something to eat, typing something on a pad, picking-up remote of television, by plucking an apple from the tree, and many other ways.

- **Smell**

It doesn't matter whether the smell is good or bad; concentrate on what nature has to offer. Identify the one you like and the one you don't. The sole purpose of doing this activity is to focus on smell, not on problems you are facing.

- **Movement**

Technically we have five senses, but dialectical behavioral therapy introduces the sense of movement. DBT proposes that a person's emotional situation can be changed by the movement. For example, taking a walk around the park or dancing on a beat which you like the most, cooking, having a phone call with wife/husband, or as simple as taking a deep breath.

Skill 4

IMPROVE the moment

Skill used to relax a person in moments of distress. In this skill, the primary goal is to use positive mental imagery to overcome or improve the current disturbing phase of life. The acronym for this skill is 'IMPROVE':

- **I** – is for **i**magery. Such as thinking about a pleasant scene of fine interaction with a loved one. Imagining that negative feelings are going away. Imagining yourself dealing comprehensively with complex situations may give you the strength and power to change the outcome of the problem.

- **M** – is for developing or crafting out the **m**eaning from a complex situation.
- P – is for prayer, which can be towards God or any higher power aiming for power and to be open at the moment. Surrender your difficulties and ask to tolerate the moments for a little longer.

- **R** – is for **r**elaxation, which can be achieved through deep breathing, which helps in calming large muscles of the body. It can be in the form of listening to a favorite song, yoga, hot bath, relaxing walk, watching a movie, or sipping a pina colada. The idea is to engage yourself in such activities that calm the psychological problems you're facing.

- **O** – is for **o**ne thing in a particular moment, meaning a person remains neutral and concentrated on the activity happening in the current moment. The idea is to stay in the moment by letting the past and future at width. A one-way focused mind helps significantly in feeling emotions less overwhelming.

- **V** – is for **v**acation, which means taking a break from a difficult situation by visualizing or doing something pleasant. This can be in the form of visiting a nice place, switching off the TV, ignoring calls, or sitting alone. After doing such activity, an individual returns

  back to life ready to take on the challenge. Unfortunately, we are not able to make a trip happen in the moment of distress.

  - **E** – is for **e**ncouragement, by interacting with an individual in a pleasant and supportive manner which helps in tackling negative and stressful situations. Encouragement never meant to always come from external sources, and it can be derived from motivating yourself by a meaningful line to you, such as

    "all is well."

Skill 5

Focusing on Pros and Cons

Sometimes it is hard to make sensible decisions when an individual is not in a wise mind. The therapy of dialectical behavior proposes the idea of weighing out the consequences of a decision by using a pros and cons list. People commonly fall into behaviors of self-destruction and harm in the moments of the emotional disparity. An individual can furnish a pros and cons list and decide whether to tolerate an urge or act on it. It can be in the form of a paper-list or visualized in mind. It's basically thinking about positive and negative things of no tolerance distress.

Skill 6

Radical Acceptance

Accepting the situation of how it is while letting go fighting and flighting reality. Often we find ourselves in an unwanted situation that we do not like or approve. In such times of difficulty, accepting the current situation as it is will allow us to feel peace and provide space to move on. This skill, radical acceptance, acknowledges that human beings have the choice, and often it's upon their to deice whether to accept the reality of the current situation or not.

- **Turning the mind**

Shifting a mind towards the stance of acceptance, which shall be exercised with radical acceptance.

➢ **Willingness vs. willfulness**

Courage and willingness to do what is effective by letting go of willful stance, which is clearly against acceptance.

Module#3

Emotional Regulation

Adults are expected to manipulate, regularize, and manage their emotions in a way that is socially acceptable as well as personally beneficial. Emotional irregularity usually occurs when an individual has not been able to control himself. In such moments, they often say or do things that they regret afterward and wish they had been able to manage those emotions. Meditation, mindfulness, and stress management are few of the techniques which help an individual in treating and tackling negative thinking patterns. Other than this, these techniques also happen to usefully provide other benefits such as empathy, the feeling of self-worth, and a positive mood swing. There are many ways to affect a person's emotional situation, but this module generally looks to reduce the power of them willfully.

Emotional regulation consists of three components triggered by emotions:

- Starting actions.
- Inhibiting actions
- Modeling responses.

very day, we, in general, come across countless emotion-provoking stimuli, and only a few do not require any action from our end. It's quite understandable on behalf of the mind to get tangled into negativity or unknowingly ignore emotions after getting simultaneous bombarding with a lot of stimuli every single day. Emotional regulation acts as a purifier that helps an individual to identify and recognize positive and important informations and motivates him/her to avoid stress or fear. Research supports that there's a strong connection between regularized emotions and distress management. Individuals with a low level of depression tend to showcase powerful emotion control and management intelligence.

6 Emotional Regulation Skills for Adults Self-regulation emphasizes the time between feelings and reactions. It gives power to an individual to take a break for a second, think about the matter, and respond rationally. For example, a child who starts fighting for small matters surely has less emotional control compared to a child who ignores or tells parents about these things.

Here are a few skills which can be useful in diminishing emotional irregularity and sustaining it during the moments to distress.

- **Self-awareness**

  It's very important to keep in mind how we are feeling and what to name such a situation. For example, when you feel disturbed, ask – am I feeling low, do I need empathy, am I deteriorating my moments, etc.

- **Mindful Awareness**

Mindfulness gives an individual the opportunity to see what's happening inside and outside. Sometimes, a simple act of breathing that is talked earlier can help in getting out of the emotional syndrome.

- **Cognitive reappraisal**

The cognitive appraisal looks to change our way of thinking. It's an important part of psychotherapies like Cognitive Behavioural Therapy (CBT), Dialectical Behavioural Therapy (DBT), and anger management. It can be performed and integrated into a patient's life by thought replacement or situational role reversals, where a patient tries to look at a situation with a whole new different perspective.

- **Adaptability**

Irregularity of emotions diminishes our chances of adaptability to life changes. We are easily distracted and fail to utilize our coping mechanisms. That's why we often start resisting changes. Objective evaluation is a fantastic and effective exercise to build adaptability. For example, when you found yourself in the moments of utter distress and emotional pain,

start thinking about how your brother would have reacted to the similar situation, what would have been your advice to him, and after visualizing this, think, are you on the same track for yourself or not.

- **Self-compassion**

Emotional regulation can be developed by giving yourself some moments every day. Telling ourselves of the skills and techniques we possess and letting our body and mind calm down can immensely change the way we feel and react to current emotions. Self-compassion hacks can be as simple as a) regular positive self-affirming, b) breathing and relaxation control, c) compassion mediation, d) gratitude journaling, e) regular self-care.

Emotional Support

Psychologists propose that everyone out in the world has the power and capacity to build positivity and avoid our minds from getting invested in negativity. Emotional support can be achieved from inside and outside: practicing mindful self-awareness and by effective interactions with others. It's okay to visit a professional therapist when an individual feels that the inner coping mechanism is failing. The therapist tries to develop a positive emotional shield that can bring out the finest version of us.

Science-based Emotion Regulation Strategies Science has introduced a bunch of ways out for emotional dysregulation. All the plan of action used for self-regulation are useful, but the complexity arises when one-self has to choose the best. Mostly researches done on this issue either concentrates on who could benefit or when it will work most effectively. Very less is talked about scientific methods that may be used to domesticize our thinking patterns. The latest studies have shed some light in this regard, and emotional regulation cannot be bound to a specific time frame or individuals and have introduced strategies that may play the role of a guide at all times.

- **Reappraisal**

Reappraisal of cognition secures long term care and offers an eternal way out to emotional distress. Through re-evaluation, depressed emotions are not forcefully eradicated or eliminated; rather, better ways to deal with them are sought. While looking for positive alternatives to the problem, a shift in mind also happens from distress and emotional pain to something pleasant.

- **Self-soothing**

The intense effects of negative thinking patterns can be minimized by self-soothing. Scientists believe that it can provide faster and efficient answers for handling emotions and thoughts as compared to self-confrontation. Several types of self-soothing exercises can be practiced in everyday life, such as loving-meditation and self-compassion. It can be achieved through music mediation, where we let ourselves relax with the sound. Reminiscence therapy also works where a person sits alone for some time and rewind back all good memories with the person whom he/she is struggling now. It works great for emotional conflicts involving people. Breathing exercises as well as simple self-care such as cooking, getting a massage,/taking a hot bath also work wonders.

- **Attention Control**

It initiates with an assessment with an aim to divert our attention away from distress and emotional pain and gives time to glance at it from a rewarding perspective. For example, a person can overpower the syndrome which abuse may inflict to him/her by thinking it as a lesson to avoid maintaining or developing any connections with unsophisticated people. As a result, one can feel accomplished at modulating response to the bad encounter and restoring mental peace.

- **Emotional Regulation Disorder**

It's a state of disrupted and weak ability to regularize and handle emotions aesthetically. It is used to describe poorly managed and deviated spiritual responses. The symptoms are as followed:

- ✓ Unforeseen and unclear anger outbursts which may get on to an individual who didn't cause any harm.

- ✓ Severe pain and illness not caused by any medical condition and stays unexplained by professionals.

- ✓ Self-destructive behavior includes intense thoughts of suicide.

- ✓ Struggling to get any sound social engagements

- ✓ Attention dysregulation, the mind stays stuck on a negative thinking pattern.
- ✓ Weak self-control and hypersensitivity

The worst part of such disorder is that it comes with mental health issues such as anxiety, stress, or extreme mood polarities. The most commonly used cure for EDD is DBT, with the assist of emotional support and cognitive strategies. The best results of interventions for the emotional regulation disorder can be achieved when the patient chooses to take charge of it soon and participates in a long-term treatment plan.

5 Tips for Developing Emotional Regulation in Children

Emotional regulation is a dire need for moral and academic nourishment in kids. Parents usually do not find the right track to teach their kids about the regulation of emotions, which results in the inevitable stress of everyday life. It's a complex task to successfully regulate emotions in someone as emotional perception and management can never be the same for two people. However, psychologists and researchers have come up with fine solutions in recent years, and here are few hacks which parents

& carers may use to foster emotional regulation in children.

- **Model the right Behaviour**

  The learning skills of a child are best utilized in the moments of observation. Practically showcasing them what to do than verbally telling is for sure far more effective and result-oriented. For example, a child plays in a sports team who treat each other equally, respectfully and resolve conflicts on the pitch without being abusive, will learn to be resilient and emotionally balanced than a child who plays and interacts with aggressive and abusive teammates. It's important to tell a child that positive thinking patterns are the 'best' and most effective way to deal with stress.

Delay response time

Encourage the child not to give instant reactions. For example, whenever a child gets dismal and angry, advise him to hold back for a while and react afterward. This little delay in response allows the fight o flight responses to calm down, and there's a probability that the child will react in a less harming way than he'd otherwise have.

- **Child's emotional vocabulary**

Self-expression is a great tool and works effectively for emotional regulation in children. Sometimes, a child encounters something which he/she is unable to explain, and the distress and frustration follow often leads to an unacceptable irksome reaction. Some psychologists advise making a chart with all the emotions written on it. Being able to identify the feelings they are experiencing makes a child more sharp and strong, as well as diminishes the chances of emotional outbursts.

- **Teaching about actions and consequences**

If a child knows what consequences will follow his/her actions, he/she will likely be careful with their acts. Teaching about action and consequences can take place anywhere, be it school or home, park or church, cinema or zoo. A child can be engaged in meaningful conversations where such learning can happen.

- **Let them detect stress**

Emotional regulation comes with an agenda of making children self-dependent as a person in the future. Certain situations, circumstances, and people provoke stress in kids. For example, ragging in school, no friends, or breaking or losing a favorite toy. If parents little time in recognizing children what depresses them, then it can be really beneficial for the future of kids. They may be aware of their stressors and make themselves ready to cope, manage, and deal with them effectively as they climb the ladder to manhood.

Emotional Regulation Modules

The third module of dialectical behavioral therapy is emotional regulation, which emphasizes teaching a patient how to cope, manage anxiety, and distressing emotions while enhancing their positive experiences. This module carries three essential emotional goals:

- Understand one's emotions
- Reduce vulnerability
- Decrease suffering

It's important to understand that distressing emotions are not phenomena that must be avoidable. Rather they're a normal part of life, and there are ways to accept and leave away feeling so that one is not controlled by them.

Understand one's emotions

The first and foremost skill in emotional regulation is to identify and name emotions. Patients are taught to use labels such as 'depressed' or ' anxious' rather than general terms because vaguely defined are pretty hard to manage. Another significant difference is of primary and secondary emotions. An initial response to a specific event is called the primary emotion, while the secondary is a reaction of one's thoughts. Secondary are generally more destructive and make a person more vulnerable to harmful behaviors. Group leaders usually discuss myths about emotions in dialectical behavioral therapy sessions. They teach that there is a misconception about the right and wrong ways to feel in a situation. Our emotions serve a purpose that alerts us that something in our environment is either problematic or beneficial. These emotions are simultaneously typified in mind blocks, which helps us while facing a similar situation in the future.

Reducing Emotional Vulnerability

The acronym for the first skill is in diminishing emotional vulnerability is "please master."

PL – is for taking care of our physical health and curing illness.

E – represents eating a balanced diet and avoiding carbohydrates enriched food.

A – is for avoiding alcohol and other drugs which injects emotional instability

S – is for getting adequate sleep **E** – is for regular exercise.

MASTER – points to do daily activities that develop competency and confidence.

This skill is developed to reduce the vulnerability of emotions, which is extracted by building positive experiences in order to balance the negativity of life. Patients are encouraged to extract one or more daily experiences that they can look upon and enjoy. It can be achieved by taking a hot bath, visiting some cool place, or watching a movie. It's essential to perform these activities with mindfulness.

Decreasing Emotional Suffering

Last part of the module consists of two skills:

- Letting go
- Taking the opposite action

The first one refers to be in the center spot of current emotion through mindfulness, naming it, and then letting it go rather than thinking about to cope or fight. It can be achieved by taking a deep breath and visualizing something pleasant.

The second one refers to engaging in such behaviors that are completely opposite to the current emotions of an individual. For example, when an individual is feeling depressed, he gets up, talks to others decently, and with a smile on his face. It's not about denying current emotions but let it go by engaging in something else.

Some of these DBT skills may feel vague to those who are unfamiliar with this particular therapy. In a group session, the therapist tries to teach skills with detail and idea of how to manifest them in practical life at the time of need. These skills provide power and strength to people to manage their emotions rather than hiding behind.

Module#4

Interpersonal Effectiveness

Our way of communicating with each other has a significant effect on the quality of our bonds. The individuals suffering from Dialectical Behavioural Therapy are taught skills to initiate and develop conversations in a thoughtful and wise manner rather than acting and reacting spontaneously due to stress or distress emotions. The key concepts of this module are the ability to ask for things and deny, when appropriate. The Dialectical Behaviour Therapy developer Dr. Marsha Linehan recognized three types of effects that must be considered in interpersonal exchanges:

- Objective
- Relationship
- Self-respect

These three factors are must be considered on priority in any circumstance. An individual seems to be more pleased when an effective interaction consists of his or her priority.

1Objective effectiveness points towards the goal of the interaction, which usually is a tangible result. Suppose, a man waits for a call from his wife when she will be working late.

2Relationship effectiveness refers to the purpose of a conflict-free relationship. In this instance, the husband might rank emotional contagiousness and polyphony as his highest priority. Oppositely, 3self-respect effectiveness might be the foremost priority if the man feels that her failure to call is disrespectful to him. DBT uses acronyms to help patients remember their skills.

DEAR MAN is an acronym used for objective effectiveness, and the skills are as stated below:

D – Describe**:** describe the situation in a comprehensive manner and free from judgment.

E – Express: express feelings, telling other one's how the circumstance makes me feel.

A – Assert: assert wishes, tell, what do you want and what you do not.

R – Reinforce: reinforce why such an outcome is desirable.

M – Mindful, be present at the moment while staying focused on the goal.

A – Appear: appear confident, with confident eye contact, tone, and posture.

N – Negotiate: be open to negotiation and give in order to get, with the rationality that both parties have valid needs. **GIVE** is an acronym for relationship effectiveness: **G** – Gentle: approach the other party in a nice, smooth, and kind manner avoiding offensive remarks.

I – Interested: act interested while listening to the other fellow without creating interruption.

V - Validate: validate and acknowledge the other fellow's feelings and opinions.

E – Easy: assume an easy manner by gently smiling and using a sophisticated tone.

Lastly, the Dialectical behavioral therapy acronym for self-respect effectiveness is **FAST**:

F - Fair: be fair to everyone including yourself to avoid resentment

A – Apologies: apologies for the minimum, take a stance only when appropriate.

S – Stick: stick to your deep-rooted values and never compromise on your dignity for the desired outcome.

T – Truthful: be truthful and avoid acting helpless to influence others

These interpersonal skills taught in DBT enhance the likelihood of pleasant outcomes doesn't matter how the individual prioritizes the skills of objective, relationship, and self-dignity for a particular interaction. When exercised efficiently, the DEAR-MAN-GIVE-FAST skills assist a man in conveying his or her needs with clarity without other individuals having to read their minds.

Taking Control of Personality Disorder

It's supported by research that DBT has been more useful than community-based treatment. It includes reducing cases of parasuicidal behaviors, enhancing adherence to therapy, and reducing the number of hospital admits. It has also been significantly efficient in co-occurring substance use disorders, binge eating, bulimia nervosa, and depression.

Dialectical behavior therapy traditionally consists of four components: (i) skills training group (ii) individual psychotherapy (iii) telephonic therapy and (iv) therapist team. The therapy of dialectical behavior can be shortened or modified according to the situation.

- **Skills Training Group**

  Concentration in such a session is on enhancing the capabilities of an individual by equipping with different behavioral skills. It takes place like a class where the teacher teaches different skillsets and assigns homework to practice them in everyday life. The group tends to meet for 2 hours a week and acquire knowledge to exercise specific skills, which are classified as mindfulness,

  distress tolerance, interpersonal effectiveness, and emotion regulation.

- **Individual Psychotherapy**

Therapists and patients are only involved in such sessions where the primary focus is on

enhancing motivation and helping the sick in applying a specific set of skills in their everyday life. The standard dialectical behavioral therapy takes place once a week for approximately 60 minutes consisting of different skill groups. There are six main areas of focus in weekly individual therapy treatment: parasuicidal behaviors, therapy-interfering behavior, behavior skills acquisition, self-respect behaviors, behaviors clashing with the standards of life, and post-trauma stress behaviors. 1Presuicidal behaviors, whether with real suicidal intent or not, are never ignored in DBT. Such behaviors are explored in detail, and focus is paid on problem-solving behaviors, tangling in the coping mechanism, and using distress-eradicating techniques. 2Therapy-interfering behaviors can happen on anyone's behalf, be it a therapist or patient. Drop-out rates can be reduced by managing therapy-interference.

3Any sort of behavior which interferes in the quality and smooth running of life such as substance abuse, high-risk sexual behaviors, job or health issues, or any illegal issue.

[4]Skills used in an individual's everyday life are called 'behavioral skills.' Skills of maintaining and learning behaviors and letting go of unhealthy and negative behaviors are taught and reinforced throughout therapy. [5]A lot of people commences for a therapy session with a trauma history. It's necessary for the therapist to address trauma history when the patient appears ready. This emphasization includes rewinding abuse, reducing labeling, and self-blame, eliminating intrusive thoughts regarding abuse and diminishing polarization of the self and the abuser. [6]Such behaviors are designed to increase the individual's ability to validate him/herself. Greater self-reliance is necessary to build. And the professional looks to reinforce and integrate self-respect behaviors throughout the session.

- **Phone Coaching**

The individual can pick his/her therapist on call whenever they're in trouble and need help. It is provided to patients to overcome difficult situations that may arise at any moment. Such calls usually happen during therapy sessions. It's usually a brief call focusing on arising issues. Such a strategy is used to minimize the reinforcement of

parasuicidal behaviors. Patients are informed as soon as therapy commences that their call
is expected before engaging in parasuicidal behavior. There's also a rule of 24-hours, which means that the sick is not allowed to call their therapist for 24 hours after committing any parasuicidal act. The rule is meant to urge the sick to seek help at the initial stage of a crisis while the therapist can assist and not after the individual has already committed or chosen maladaptive behavior.

- **Therapist Consultation Team**

These teams are developed to assist therapists in staying committed, energetic, motivated, and competent so they can provide fine treatment to their cases. Such teams usually get together for once in a week to discuss each client's care. This seven-day meeting consists of all therapists who are currently providing Dialectical Behavioural Therapy. Due to any reason, if a group setting is not possible, therapists are urged to be part of some consultation...

Components of DBT

Dialectical Behavior Therapy is a method employed by therapists to focus on the social and emotional aspects of a client's mental condition in order to treat it. It was first used when people with Borderline Personality Disorder (BPD) tried to commit suicide. This method was used to treat these patients effectively. Further, DBT can also be used to treat other disorders such as depression, substance abuse, PTSD (Post Traumatic Stress disorder).

The Dialectical term in DBT means the integration of opposites. This means that the client and the patient have to work effectively together to produce effective results. The therapist is taught skills through which he can help the patient to deals with his emotions effectively. The therapist helps the patients realize practical and achievable goals according to the severity of their condition and helps them set a path to achieve those goals. The therapist helps the client to accept and adapt to change.

Components of DBT

There are four basic components of DBT:

1. Skills Training Group

2. Individual Treatment

3. DBT Phone Coaching

4. Consultation Team

5. Skill Training Group

6.

7. This technique aims at enhancing a client's behavioral skills through different techniques. It is similar to group therapy, but rather than talking about how they feel, and they are taught to deal with their emotions effectively. The therapist teaches them techniques related to improving their behavioral skills set. In addition to teaching them, the therapist also assigns them to practice these techniques at home, in their daily life. This helps them incorporate effective techniques to help them deal with their disorder. Group therapy lasts about 2-3 hours per week. This is a 24-week therapy that can be repeated and extended to a one year program. Every group has its own schedule and is dealt with accordingly. The schedules are set to impart skills in the individual effectively. These skills are set according to the skills or traits an individual might be missing in their personality normally. These group sessions have proven to be an effective component for DBT.

8.

9. Individual Treatment

10.

11. Sometimes the therapist might encounter an individual with social phobia or any similar disorder. Such individuals cannot be effectively treated in groups; thus, individual treatments are advised for such patients. Individual therapy aims at helping the individual to attain confidence in addition to other skills. This is an effective method, as well as an approach that is preferred by clients that like to be treated in privacy.

These one-one sessions help the individuals develop skills that help them to not only deal with their issues but to lead normal lives. These sessions can be held about once every week and for about 60 minutes each. Once the individual starts gaining confidence, the concept of group training can also be introduced in addition to the individual treatments. This helps as the individual does not feel left out but feels connected to other people that have faced similar disorders.

DBT Phone Coaching

DBT phone coaching provides mobility to the technique. This method allows the individual to contact their corresponding therapist at any time. The individual can consult and gain guidance through any tough condition. This method is also very effective as the therapist has a better understanding of the client's disorder and how efficiently the client is dealing with the faced problems. Further, it helps the therapist analyze how effective the skills are proving to be in the client's life. In the case where a person shows the difficulty in adapting any skill, the therapists can look for an alternative method to help the patient deal with the problem more effectively. DBT phone coaching can be done in addition to the skills training and individual training for fruitful results.

DBT therapist consultation

In some cases, a single therapist fails to guide his patients due to the severity or complexity of the condition. To effectively deal with the condition, the patient and therapist can consult different doctors regarding the case. This will be helpful as the therapist will remain dedicated to treating the patient, and the patient will get effective treatment to produce better results. Multiple therapists can work together on treating the case and come with a schedule to impart skill sets, the individual requires. This way, the patient gets the best possible treatment. Further, the individual can be suggested individual treatments and skills training. All these things can be planned and effectively dealt with through multiple therapist consultation.

All these components can be effectively included in treating the individual.

DBT SKILLS

There are four basic skills that are taught to therapists in DBT. These skills include:

Acceptance Oriented Skills

The first step to solving any problem is acknowledging the fact that you have to deal with the problem. Through Acceptance oriented skills, the individuals are taught to accept their present condition and acknowledge all the emotions without trying to manipulate or suppress them in any way. Thus, the individual is taught to deal with distress mindfully.

Change Oriented Skills

Once the individual has acknowledged the fact that they require help for their condition, they will show less resistance to the change that comes in their life. Small changes can be incorporated into the individual's routine to help them deal better with their condition. The individual is taught to effectively regulate their emotions and thus help them develop good interpersonal skills.

Thus four basic skills are practiced using DBT:

Mindfulness

This skill requires the person to be fully aware of the current moment and act according to that instead of worrying about the future.

Distress Tolerance

DBT is used to treat severe conditions such as BPD. The main aim of the therapy is to help the patients deal effectively with stressful situations. Tips and tricks are provided to help them remain calm through stressful situations.

Effective interpersonal skills

Helping an individual improve their personality, means helping them improve their interpersonal skills. Improving interpersonal skills means helping the individual identify situations where the individual might feel uncomfortable and act accordingly.
Teaching the individual to say no in situations where the individual might not feel comfortable considering self-respect

and relationships with others is a significant part of the treatment.

Regulation of emotions

Another aim of the therapy is to help the individual regulate his/her emotions effectively. This means not letting their emotions take over and finding effective methods to manipulate their emotions effectively.

All these skills can be developed effectively to ensure successful results through DBT.

How does the treatment work?

DBT can opt-in cases where the patient might be suffering from more than one disorder. In this case, the treatment has to be scheduled according to the severity of the conditions. The therapist needs to map an effective schedule where the therapist can target each disorder and try to deal with each disorder individually effectively. The order in which the treatment should be done should be as :

The most important things to be dealt with are situations where people might threaten their own life. These conditions

can lead to suicide. Such conditions should be the first preference to deal with.
The next thing to be given importance is the client's/patient's reaction to the therapy and whether the patient is showing any signs of resisting the therapy. This can be noted in the individual's behavior, such as the individual might not cooperate with the therapist; the individual might show up late at the appointments or might not show up at all. These behavioral patterns need to be noticed and taken care of for effective treatment.

The next target can be identifying where the individual falls behind in daily life, thus deteriorating their standard of living in any way. These can be identified through problems in the individual's social relations or financial crisis and should be taken into serious account, to ensure effective treatment.

The last target of the therapy can be helping the individual to replace skills that are not effective in any manner with skills that prove to be effective. For the development of the individuals' personality, it is necessary that the individual tries to replace ineffective skills with effective skills to ensure efficient results.

Stages of treatment

DBT can be divided into four stages of treatment. Each stage has its own importance and priority to be dealt with. The therapist defines these stages and, thus, effectively treats the individual.

Stage 1

DBT is used to treat individuals suffering from extreme conditions such as that of suicide. Such people have the tendency of harming not only themselves but others around them, suggesting that their behavior is out of their control. Thus, the first stage involves helping the patient overcome this stage.

Stage 2

The next thing that is to be treated can be targeted is the individual's emotional experiences. Some individuals have their behavior under control but are still unable to comprehend what they feel effective. They can be considered as depressed due to multiple reasons such as past trauma. Stage 2 aims at helping the individual to regain emotional experience.

Stage 3

Stage 3 aims at bringing these individuals towards a normal life. Helping them develop believes and morals that aims to help them define their life goals, build self-respect, along with this help them lead an ordinary life.

Stage 4

Certain individuals have full control over their emotions and are able to lead normal lives. However, it lacks experiencing emotions or life at its fullest. Stage 4 aims at helping people achieve a feeling of fulfillment.
Each stage has its own importance, and if the requirements of each stage are met effectively, this can produce fruitful results for DBT.

Different techniques can be used by the therapist according to the needs of their patients to effectively deal with the disorders or the problems the individual might be facing. Thus DBT is an extensive procedure, with effective components, skills, and stages to help the patient recover and come back to normal .

Who benefits from DBT?

Dialectical Behavioral Therapy is an effective method to help people suffering from mental disorders. According to research, when an individual lacks a certain skill set, they are more prone to mental disorders. For example, people who have Borderline personality disorder lack basic emotional regulation skills. Through DBT treatment, these individuals develop these skills and thus effectively overcome the disorder. Thus, the main aim of DBT is to improve the individuals' skill set to help them effectively deal with their disorder.

Through research, it has been proved that DBT has been the most successful treatment method for people who have Borderline personality disorder. However, DBT can be used as an effective treatment for other mental disorders too.

Some conditions that can be effectively dealt with using DBT can be suggested as follows:

1. People have Borderline personality disorder, in addition to behavior patterns suggesting that the individual has self-harming or suicidal behavior. Other than that it can be used to treat individuals that are a victim of substance abuse. People suffering from Cluster B personality disorders can be treated effectively using DBT.
2. Individuals showing self-harming traits or any other personality disorder can also be treated through DBT.

3. DBT can be used to effectively treat patients suffering from Attention Deficit hyperactive Disorder (ADHD).

4. DBT can also be used to treat children that have been subjected to abuse or violence and maybe suffering from post-traumatic stress.

5. It may also be used to deal with depression, whether it is mild or chronic depression.

6. DBT is used in treating Bipolar Disorder

7. DBT is used in treating Transdiagnostic Emption Dysregulation

8. DBT is used in treating children suffering from extreme behavioral or emotional dysregulation.

9. DBT is used in treating an eating disorder.

DBT aims at treating each disorder individually and effectively by making certain schedules for the individuals to follow according to their condition effectively. Each individual has their own schedule and thus can work on the skills set he/she requires effectively.

Similar to other Borderline personality disorder, other treatments can also prove to be successful by aiming at helping the individual attain certain skills. Some of the disorders that can be treated through DBT can be observed as follows:

Dialectical behavior therapy and Post Traumatic Stress

Post-Traumatic Stress might be experienced by an individual that might have faced violence, abuse, or any natural disaster. Sometimes the effect of the trauma wears off, whereas, at other times, it may develop into post-traumatic stress. DBT was initially developed for Borderline personality disorder, but it can be used in combination with other techniques to treat PTSD effectively. The skills that DBT aims at developing are to help patients suffering from post-traumatic stress are increases emotional regulation, in which the individuals are taught to deal with their emotions effectively by manipulating them accordingly. Finally, it helps the individual to avoid and eliminate destructive traits from the individual's personality.

DBT addresses the individual's concerns by removing any stressful environment for the individual. By being considerate about what the individual wants, a trusting relationship is built between the therapist and the individual. The individual learns to manipulate their emotions and effectively practice mindfulness along with other DBT skills.

Dialectical behavior therapy and Depression DBT was not structured to deal with depression, but with the combination of some effective techniques, it can be done so. DBT aims at developing certain skills in an individual that help the individual overcome certain mental disorders.

People suffering from depression often feel worthless; thus, they require validation or acknowledgment for the things they do. Further, they have a low tolerance for certain conditions. DBT has certain techniques that help in achieving both the targets effectively and thus prove to be a healthy treat, as it helps the person to be sure about themself. DBT also helps individuals to establish a healthy living environment for themselves.

The treatment not only aims at boosting the individuals' confidence but also helps the individual to regulate their emotions. The therapist often suggests individuals keep diaries; this is done to keep track of their emotions. Once the individuals start noticing repetitive emotional patterns as a response, the individuals can effectively regulate their emotions. This can be done by effectively keeping track of one's emotions.

Dialectical behavior therapy and Bipolar Disorder

Bipolar disorder is also a type of depression that can be effectively treated through DBT. In addition to the methods suggested above, practicing DBT skills such as mindfulness helps the person overcome bipolar personality disorder.

DBT (Dialectical personality disorder) was initially created to treat people who have Borderline personality disorder. Over the years, multiple techniques have been developed that help the therapist treat other disorders in addition to BDP. This is done through a careful combination of DBT with other effective treatment methods. Each one of the components, as well as the skills used in the DBT treatment, proves to be beneficial for the patient.

Benefits of DBT

Dialectical behavior therapy was a treatment used to treat borderline personality. Over the course of time, it has been used to treat other conditions through some useful combinations.

Some disorders that DBT has proven to be successful for:

Borderline personality disorder

BPD is the condition that affects how an individual thinks about themselves. Intense emotions in this regard are characterized to be BPD. This does affect not only the individual's personality but also affects their relations with other people. DBT helps people develop certain skills to develop their personalities effectively.

Eating Disorders

Cognitive behavior therapy (CBT) is considered when treating patients suffering from eating disorders. However, CBT does not work in every case, and thus DBT is thought to be a good alternative while treating eating disorders. Eating disorders can be caused by intense emotions leading to food cravings or ignoring any food at all. In such scenarios, DBT helps the individual to manage and control their emotions effectively. The treatment also aims at proving healthy coping mechanisms to people suffering from the disease.

However, DBT is considered to be a better treatment while treating eating disorders in patients with bulimia nerves or binge eating, rather than treating people with anorexia nervosa.

Suicidal Feeling

Most people that have the tendency to act suicidal thoughts may lack basic coping skills with difficult situations and thus are unable to deal with them effectively. DBT helps individuals develop the required skill set to cope with suicidal thoughts effectively.

Benefits of DBT in treating Addiction programs

Treating people suffering from addiction problems can be tricky as the therapist has to move according to the patient's pace and capacity to adapt to the change. The therapist has to acknowledge that he/she might have to face certain problems if the patient cannot cope up with the treatment.

Many individuals are sent to rehabilitation centers to recover from addictions programs where most of them might visit the place because they want to seek treatment; many would not have the same agenda. Thus the therapist should monitor each patient individually and treat them accordingly to get productive results. If a patient is resistant to participating actively in the treatment, the therapist should try to make the person acknowledge the disorder or problem at hand, and help them achieve a solution according to their will.

The therapist makes an effort to recognize the emotional patterns of their patients and help them cope with their condition. The main aim of DBT being helping the patient improve their quality of living through skills and tips that would help them avoid impulsive behavior.

Some case scenarios can be discussed in accordance with the target that therapists wan to achieve are:

1. People that do not feel confident in their own skin sometimes feel depressed and thus get addicted to drugs and other substances. DBT helps an individual to regain their confidence and feel comfortable in what they do. It aims at making them feel normal by accepting themselves for who they are. Once the individual has accepted their disorder, it becomes a lot easy to treat them. Thus DBT aims at making people feel confident about themselves, leading to reduce depression and other associated self-harming activities.

2. A person may feel the need for substance abuse if he/she is subjected to any uncomfortable trigger. The therapist helps the individual identify their triggers. Once the trigger has been identified, the therapist can suggest the family to either help the individual avoid the trigger or cope with the trigger effectively. This helps the individual

develop healthy coping mechanisms in response to the triggers.

3. DBT does not only help the individual develop skills to treat the disorder, but helps incorporate these skills in their daily life. These skills help the individual not only to increase their quality of life but also help the individuals to develop positive behavior traits to their benefit.

4. Addiction is basically associated with substance abuse. Once the treatment starts, it can help the individual to reduce substance abuse and lead a healthy living style.

5. Through the therapy keeping, both the therapist and the client to remain motivated to carry out the process are integral to get fruitful results. Through DBT, activities are carried involving full input from both the

   therapist and the client. By providing full input to the treatment, the patient does not feel that all his /her efforts are going into vain and continue with the treatment without looking back to substance use as an excuse to avoid treatment.

6. The main aim can be helping the individuals realize that substance abuse is not the only solution to their problems. Further, they are introduced to tricks that can help them remain calm and composed during their craving.

All these benefits can be achieved through DBT treatments for addiction problems.

Some more generic benefits of DBT are:

Improves relationships:

People suffering from mental illnesses need a strong support system to go through the process. They often need people to believe in them so that they can believe in themselves. Most treatments don't acknowledge the fact that people who have mental illness need support to go through the process. DBT is a treatment that effectively keeps this fact in check and incorporates this in the patient's schedule.

The therapist considers the patient's family affiliations and treats accordingly. The therapists can advise the precautionary family steps to follow in order to avoid any set back in the process. The treatment aims at building healthy relationships as it reflects strong social values on the individuals' part.

Improving skillset

The main aim of DBT is to improve an individual's skills to overcome mental disorders. However, the skill set is not only imparted, keeping in mind the disorder. The skillset is incorporated into the individual's daily routine and becomes a healthy practice after the individual has fully recovered.

Some examples of the skills that the individuals can practice in their daily life, irrespective whether the patients are ill or not can be:

1. **Mindfulness**

   Being mindful helps a person to remain and analyze the present effectively rather than dwell on the future. This trait should be practiced by everyone for effective working in daily life.

2. **Tolerance for stress**

   Anger and stress management can happen to anyone, and not every individual is capable of handling anger and stress in an effective manner. DBT helps an individual attain skills and trips that help them remain calm in stressful situations.

Thus DBT skills do not only help the patient while being treated but help the individual throughout their life.

Setting better living standards:

One of the main aims of DBT is helping individuals set better standards of living. This is done to ensure a tough time. The therapists acknowledge what condition the individual is facing and deals with it in an effective manner. The therapist makes the individual feel accepted in society and thus boosts the individuals' confidence and, thus, the quality of life for the individual. The therapist understands and helps the individual through a tough time.

It is the responsibility of the therapist to make the individual feel comfortable in his/her own skin. Once the patient has successfully acknowledged the problem and the fact that many people might be going through the same process, the treatment becomes easier and more effective. The therapist instills skills that help the individual raise their quality of living.

The main aim of DBT can be recognized as not only helping people develop skills, just for the sake of treatment, learn to make those skills a habit in their daily life.

Advantages of dialectical behavior therapy:

The following are some of the benefits of DBT:

- Decreasing high risk suicidal and self-harming behavior.
- Decreasing therapy interfering behaviors
- For reducing behaviors that interfere with the quality of life.
- Learning and mastering behavior skills for mood-independent life choices
- Decreasing symptoms related to trauma, stress, anxiety, and depression
- Enhancing and sustaining self-respect
- Assistance with goal setting to create a life worth living.

By focusing on facts rather than emotions or value judgments such as right/wrong or fair/unfair, DBT residents enhance their abilities to respond positively and productively, without descending into self-blame or other destructive thoughts and behaviors.

Disadvantages of DBT:

Many kinds of research suggest that DBT is an effective treatment for mental health problems. But DBT has some limitations. All the research that yet done on DBT shows the effectiveness of small sizes on the specific sectors of the mental health population. Some experts argue, more research should be done to determine if DBT works well for different or more complex mental health concerns.

DBT uses a detailed manual and solid training to implement. In many research studies where DBT found to be successful, the DBT therapists were doctor-level therapists or higher. The developer, Marsha Linehan, trained most. The therapy does not necessarily indicate a weakness in the version of the treatment itself but emphasizes the in-depth amount of training required to deliver the facilities as designed. Increasing the availability of comprehensive training is useful for the community mental health organizations. Some DBT research trails last up to a year.

But, it's not yet examined whether the therapeutic gains last beyond the post-treatment follow up Interviews. Due to the persistent nature of the conditions treated, the field of DBT could benefit from more research by measuring treatment gains.

DBT emotion regulation and distress tolerance

DBT SKILLS

There are four basic skills that are taught to therapists in DBT. These skills include:

Acceptance Oriented Skills

The first step to solving any problem is acknowledging the fact that there is a problem to deal with. Through acceptance oriented skills, the individuals learn to accept and acknowledge their current condition instead of avoiding, suppressing, or manipulating their feelings. Thus, the individual is taught to deal with distress mindfully.

Change Oriented Skills

Once the individual has acknowledged the fact that they require help for their condition, they will show less resistance to the treatment and the change that comes with the treatment in their life. Small changes can be included in the individual's routine to help them cope better with their condition. The individual is taught to effectually regulate their emotions and thus help them develop good interpersonal skills.

Thus four basic skills are practiced using DBT:

Mindfulness

This skill requires the person to be fully aware of the present and act according to that instead of worrying about the future.

Distress Tolerance

DBT is used to treat severe conditions such as BPD. The main aim of the therapy is to help the patients deal effectively with situations that prove to be stressful. Tips and techniques are provided to help them remain calm through stressful situations.

Effective interpersonal skills

Helping an individual improve their personality, means helping them ultimately improve their interpersonal skills. Improving interpersonal skills means helping the individual identify scenarios, where the individual might feel uncomfortable. Teaching the individual to say no in situations where the individual might not feel comfortable considering self-respect and relationships is one of the aims of incorporating DBT skills.

Regulation of emotions

Another aim of the therapy is to help the individual regulate their emotions successfully. This means not letting their emotions take over and finding effective methods to manipulate their emotions accordingly.

All these skills can be developed effectively to ensure successful results through DBT. Let us discuss some of these skills in detail:

]

Regulation of Emotions

Regulation of emotions is one of the main achievements attained through DBT for the successful treatment of any mental disorder. An individual that has the ability to control his/her emotions can control their actions accordingly.

Emotional Regulation helps the individual recognize their emotions, which situations cause what kind of emotions, and how to deal with them effectively. Once an individual has control over his/her emotions, they become less vulnerable to unwanted conditions. Further, they can control what emotions they need to process and which emotions they can ignore. This helps improve individuals' mental health.

Why do we need Emotion Regulation?

Regulating one's emotions can help the individual go through multiple difficult circumstances. People with mental disorders often have triggers that trigger a certain behavior; once the individual has recognized the behavior, he/she can take precautionary measures to avoid the trigger or deal with it effectively. Recognizing a trigger requires the individual to recognize and understand the emotion associated with that activity if a person does not feel comfortable during any activity that can be suggested as a trigger.

Once recognized, certain steps can be taken to regulate emotions to bring out positive behaviors on the individual's part. Thus emotional regulation helps an individual acknowledge and control their emotions in an effective and positive manner.

Understanding One's emotion

Recognizing one's emotions can be tricky. Every emotion that an individual feels has its own purpose. Many times, a situation might seem right, but the individual might feel something off about the situation. This feeling is known as gut feeling and is the body's way of telling whether something is right or wrong. Most of the time, an individual is unable to identify this feeling as right or wrong. For example, an individual might meet a stranger. The stranger might be cheery and a delight to meet, but something about the stranger seems to be off. This instinct is specifically called gut instinct and can be right or wrong, depending on different scenarios.

Sometimes what an individual feels might be projected through his/her facial expressions or body language. Thus an individual needs to be observant about small things such as that of body language if he/she feels something off about someone.

Emotions and consideration can be taken as a two-way street. If a person cares for someone, the other person might reciprocate the feeling. However, if the individual acts bitterly around other individuals, he/she might be treated badly.
Thus, individuals' emotions should be in their control so as they do not hurt anybody if they don't want to be hurt by anybody.

An individual's body keeps them safe from dangerous situations. The flight and fight response can be considered in this situation.

According to this phenomenon, an individual's body is able to act according to an active emotion.

Flight means avoiding the situation, on the whole, whereas fight would mean confronting the situation. Regulating one's emotion through this phenomenon helps an individual identify whether the individual should avoid or confront the situation. This is often done to avoid triggers in cases of mental disorders. An important am of gaining emotional regulation is identifying whether the emotion is worth giving. An individual should try to identify every emotion they feel, whether good or bad, and then decide how they want to react as a response, or if they want to react as a response to the emotion at all.

An important trick that is often practiced while imparting emotional regulation is **ABC Please Skills**. These skills help a person to become less vulnerable to unwanted emotions.

A stands for accumulating positive experiences. Participating in positive activities and gaining positive experiences sometimes help an individual to remain positive and have an optimistic approach towards life. When an individual has more positive experiences as compared to negative experiences, they will tend to live their life more efficiently.

B stands for building mastery. It is believed that no human is perfect, and every individual needs to keep on improving and adapting to new methods and techniques to succeed in society.

Keeping this thing in mind, an individual should constantly work on their skills and talents. This helps the person feel motivated and committed towards life as well as confident about them. Once an individual is confident, this helps him/her to succeed in many domains of their lives.

C stands for Cope Ahead. This means preparing in advance for situations, an individual knows, he/she might get uncomfortable in normally. Preparing to cope with these situations helps the individual to deal with these situations in a more effective manner. This practice will help the individual built a healthy coping mechanism for difficult situations ahead of time.

PLEASE represent a set of activities that should be done to ensure good mental health. These activities include:

- Treating Physical Illness
- Balanced eating
- Avoiding Mood altering Drugs
- Good Sleep
- Exercise

All these activities ensure a healthy physical routine, as it is tied directly to the individual's mental health. Caring for one's health helps the individual to remain focused in their life. However, a person that often remains sick is more prone to negative thoughts as compared to an individual that is healthy.

All these skills and techniques are used by therapists while training patients who have any mental illness.

The strategy of the opposite action

Each emotion and individual feels it urges the individual to some action. If an action is not according to a certain emotion, the strategy of the opposite action can be used. For example, when an individual feels happy, they smile, they feel proud when they have done something good. However, some actions might not align with the emotions associated with them, such as an individual might fear to speak in public. Speaking in public is not a fearful act. As the emotion does not align with the action, the strategy can be applied. The individual can start off by talking in front of two people and thus increase the crowd over time; this will help the individual regulate negative emotions and do something productive.

Emotional regulation helps an individual not only to identify the emotions and the urge associated with them but also helps to deal with the emotions effectively. Further, it helps identify which emotions are worth acting upon and which are not worth wasting energy over.

Distress tolerance

Through an individual's life, an individual can face a crisis of various multitudes. It can be as small as a long line of traffic or disturbing as the death of a loved one. Due to these, a person might feel stresses the majority of the time. DBT aims at helping individuals to deal with the crisis effectively.

Some tricks that are adapted by therapists to help individuals deal with distress can be suggested below:

Sometimes a person might be facing extreme mental pressure, to the point of breakdown; to help a person remain calm during such conditions, DBT has introduced TIPP.

TIPP stands for Temperature, Intense Exercise, and Paced breathing, and paired muscle relaxation.

Temperature

During stressful or anger igniting situations, an individual's body might feel hot as compared to normal conditions. Changing or regulating body temperature helps. The individual can splash their face with cold water, or stand in from of an AC. These practices will help the individual to cool down and remain composed during the situation.
Emotional regulation helps an individual not only to identify the emotions and the urge associated with them but also helps to deal with the emotions effectively. Further, it helps identify which emotions are worth acting upon and which are not worth wasting energy over.

Distress tolerance

Through an individual's life, an individual can face a crisis of various multitudes. It can be as small as a long line of traffic or disturbing as the death of a loved one. Due to these, a person might feel stresses the majority of the time. DBT aims at helping individuals to deal with the crisis effectively.

Some tricks that are adapted by therapists to help individuals deal with distress can be suggested below:

Sometimes a person might be facing extreme mental pressure, to the point of breakdown; to help a person remain calm during such conditions, DBT has introduced TIPP.

TIPP stands for Temperature, Intense Exercise, and Paced breathing, and paired muscle relaxation.

Temperature

During stressful or anger igniting situations, an individual's body might feel hot as compared to normal conditions. Changing or regulating body temperature helps. The individual can splash their face with cold water, or stand in from of an AC. These practices will help the individual to cool down and remain composed during the situation.

Intense exercise

Intense exercise helps a person regulate intense emotions. If a person is upset, it is advised to indulge themselves in activities where the individual would feel exhausted. This is because, once the person is exhausted, the severity of the upsetting emotion subsides. Thus exercising, even as small as a sprint, helps an individual to cool down.

Paced Breathing

Therapists often suggest various breathing exercises to deal with anger and stress issues. There are many breathing exercises that can help the person to remain calm; one such technique is called "Box Breathing." According to the technique, the individual needs to take in air for 4 seconds and breathe out for 4 seconds, i.e., each breath is for four seconds. The individual needs to focus himself on the breathing to remain calm is; this will distract the individual from the upsetting thought and remain calm.

Paired Muscle Relaxation

This technique works by the individual tightening on a pair of muscles, holding the tension for about 5 seconds, and then letting the muscles relax. This will release oxygen in the individual's body and help the individual to remain calm and composed during stressful situations.

TIPP will not only help the individual to remain calm but will help the individual to practice mindfulness while taking decisions according to their emotions.

Another technique that can be used by DBT therapists is **ACCEPT**. It helps the individual to control their emotions until the individual has a plausible solution for the problem

A stands for activities. A person can indulge in any activity while coming up with the solution. The activities can be such as reading, exercising, or cooking. This activity will help the individual to keep their mind off the negative thought.

C stands for Contributing. Any contribution can be considered as a part of the therapy. This will help the individual in two ways; it will help keep the individual's mind off the negative, though, as well as help the individual to feel good about them. These activities can be cooking dinner and inviting a neighbor to share it.

C stands for Comparison. Most therapists advise not to compare a healthy person to a person facing any illness. However, individuals suffering from a negative thought can compare to situations where the individual has dealt with worse situations and made the most out of them. If an individual considers the current situation to be the worse, he/she can compare themselves with people suffering from the same condition in much worse circumstances. The aim of this activity is not to make the person feel bad about themselves, but to help the person feel good about how far they have come. **E** stands for emotion. In DBT, a person is taught to regulate their emotions effectively. The individual can invoke opposite emotions to negative thoughts. This helps them remain distracted and happy. For example, if an individual is feeling depressed, they can go for a walk or look at puppy pictures to lighten the mood and remain calm.

P stands for Push away. Pushing away from the thought for some time can benefit the individual. The individual can push away the negative thought and remain distracted. However, the individual should realize that though the emotion/thought is pushed away, for now, it needs to be dealt with in the future.

T stands for thoughts. Trying to manipulate one's thoughts can be tricky but not impossible. An individual wants to replace negative thoughts with positive ones. This will happen only by indulging in games and other constructive activities.

S stands for sensations. The individual can indulge in soothing activities that can help relax their senses. These activities can be taking a snack, watching a good movie, or even taking a lavender bath. Once the individual is calm again, they can deal with the situation in a more effective manner.

DBT for Substance Abusers

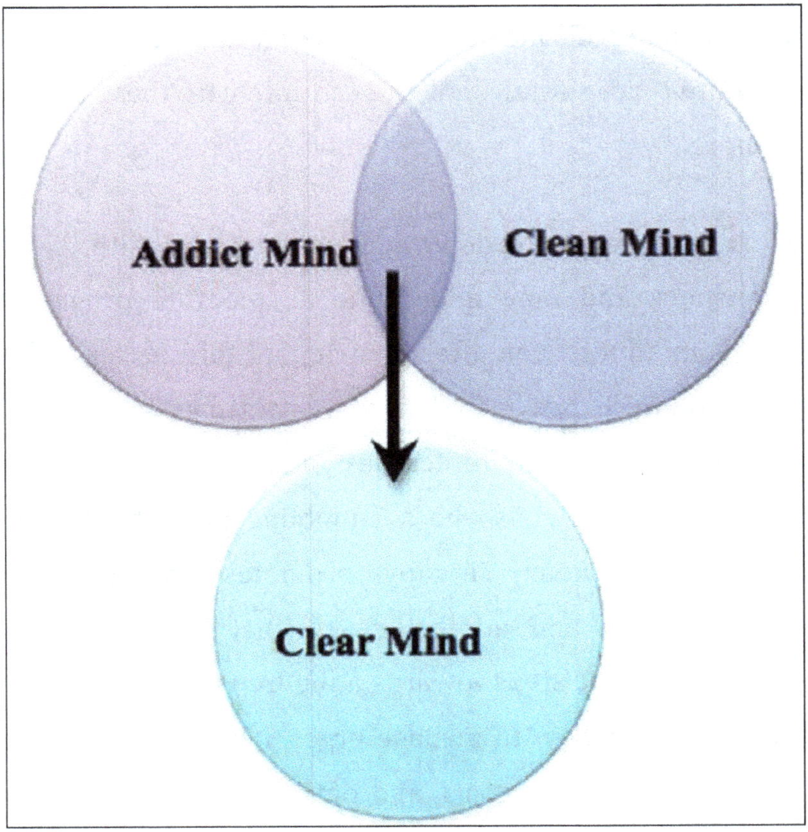

Dialectical Behavioural Therapy is an effective and dynamic source for addiction treatment. Such sessions help a person negotiate and overcome harming, substance-abusing behaviors, damage inflicting emotions, and negative thinking patterns. The therapist provides positive behaviors that build a concrete foundation for recovery success opposing the negativity of the current situation. Addiction is a result of dysfunctional emotions and self-harming behaviors. The emotional, physical, and mental distress and instability caused by repetitive drug or alcohol use can intensify these patterns even more.

Such damage can take down an individual's health, tarnish relationships, and may undermine a smoothly progressing career. Sometimes, even after knowing all this, it can be hard for a person to change and adapt to new settings. In addition to this, some people find difficulties in accepting the current situation, which can also be a stumbling block to recovery. Dialectical Behaviour Therapy promotes an equilibrium between change and acceptance so that an individual is emancipate to take steps towards a life free from drug use. An individual learns how to manage urges, healthy emotions, set positive and affirming goals, and develop relapse prevention skills. These changes create fine mind-body-spirit balance and develop sobriety.y

Dialectical Behavioural Therapy was introduced by Dr. Marsha Linehan to cure borderline personality disorders. However, it has been utilized as a cure for substance abuse disorders and different forms of mental illness. Therapy can take place in an outpatient or inpatient setting, depending upon the circumstances. An inpatient drug treatment generally offers more intensive therapies and opportunities for rehabbing and healing than does outpatient care. Co-operation and bond between therapist and patient must be of an aesthetic nature. It's generally difficult to form such a partnership at the initial stages of dialectical behavioral therapy. As soon as rehab begins, dialectical behavioral therapy encourages complete temperance. It is a very intimidating prospect for a new-comer at recovery. DBT segregates long term sobriety into smaller and more easily achieved goals. Therapists often suggest an individual set a small goal, such as being nice and sophisticated with the tone for an hour, day, or a week. Once the person has successfully achieved a particular goal, the therapist renews it and begin again. He/she keeps gaining stability and moves closer to long-term temperance as time passes.

DBT targets a few behaviors that can significantly improve a person's chance of recovery as the therapy progresses.

- ✓ Reducing withdrawal symptoms
- ✓ Reducing temptations and cravings for relapse

- ✓ Removing people, places or events which triggers drug abusement Overcoming thinking patterns that encourage drug abuse

- ✓ Reinforcing and reintegrating healthy relationships, environment, and behaviors that encourage sobriety

The primary goal of DBT is to assist a person in developing a "clear mind." In such circumstances, an individual stays concentrated on their recovery goals while also poking an eye for potential threats to their sobriety. Dialectical Behaviour Therapy deteriorates long-term sobriety into smaller, more easily obtained goals. Addiction can make it complex for an individual to take care of themselves. Maintaining quality behaviors and making healthy choices can be difficult for a person who is addicted to alcohol or drugs. Many drug or alcohol abusers find out the need for having a certain life skill, which they may not have, or they may need improvement, at the time of arriving for therapy. A therapist of Dialectical Behaviour Therapy assists a patient in recognizing what's missing in their life or on what areas of life they need to work. After the recognization of loophole areas, they work together as a team to develop an arsenal of life skills that helps to cope and manage negative thinking patterns. Sometimes, the way a person, especially a drug abuser, reacts to a situation that can make it worse. It becomes clear and evident when an individual's patterns of thinking and judging are clouded by the influence of alcohol or drugs. Such instances are tackled by personalized skills, which helps a patient in managing negativity.

While dialectical behavior therapy treats borderline personality disorders, it has shown significant promise in treating:

- ✓ Substance abuse (drugs or alcohol)
- ✓ Attention-deficit hyperactivity disorder (ADHD)
- ✓ Bipolar disorder
- ✓ Bulimia
- ✓ Binge-eating disorder
- ✓ Depression
- ✓ Post-traumatic disorder

In DBT, a therapist of the patient is the primary therapy provider. The therapist is responsible for furnishing and smoothly running the treatment plan for the concerned individual. The plan usually consists of five important functions:

- ✓ Improving an individual's instincts to change
- ✓ Increasing an individual's capabilities
- ✓ Generalizing latest behaviors
- ✓ Environment structuring
- ✓ Increasing therapist motivation and capability

These functions are delivered through four different modes in outpatient therapy: group skills training, individual therapy, telephonic therapy, and therapy for the therapist.

It's difficult to draw drug-abusing individuals into treatment. Although few easily get tangled to treatment, others behave like butterflies, frequently flying up and down of the therapist's grip. Typical butterfly problems are epidemic involvement in therapy, failure to participate in the session, and eventually early termination from therapy. The DBT takes the form of thrust for instant termination of drug abuse (change) while also inculcating the fact that if a relapse occurs, it does not mean the failure of therapy on behalf of the patient or therapist (acceptance). The dialectical behavior therapy approach, therefore, goes for the elimination of abstinence with problem-solving and nonjudgmental responses to relapse, which include techniques of diminishing the dangers of infection and overdose. DBT cures an inclination towards substance abuse as a problem to solve, rather than to think it as a sick person's inadequacy or therapy failure. When a person relapses into drug use, the therapist guides to do a behavioral analysis of the circumstances, events, or people, which led to substance abuse and noting down everything which may prove useful in such future situations. There's a common misunderstanding regarding the scope of abstinence required in DBT. In DBT, the therapist studies the scope of abstinence appropriate for every single patient based on a detailed assessment and three ruling principles:

- ✓ Focusing on the primary drug(s) of abuse, which is those that are inflicting the major self-harm to a patient according to the individual's history of abuse and behavioral analysis.

- ✓ Focus on other drugs that look to reliably rash the use of the primary drug of abuse.
- ✓ Certainty about life goals attainability.

Patients with drug abuse disorder and BPD generally have myriad problem behaviors, including self-harm and suicide inclination behaviors, in addition to those linked with drug abuse. Patients with SUD usually commences DBT in a behavioral state called 'addict mind.' They are practically and emotionally controlled by drugs. After going through the initial stages of DBT, they get a state termed as "clean mind." They are free from drugs, but immunity for future relapses stays active dependant upon circumstances. After getting through this stage, an individual finds a third state called "clear mind." The patient enjoys life free from drugs while staying fully aware and vigilant about the situation, which may lead to drug use.

The phenomenon of substance dependence in individuals with personality disorder poses risks and challenges for both parties, patients, and therapists. Dr. Marsha Linehan developed Dialectical Behaviour Therapy for chronically parasuicidal individuals with BPD. Certain interventions are adapted, including drug-specified behavioral targets for curing drug use problem, dialectical abstinence, and a set of attachment strategies for developing a powerful therapeutic relationship Dialectical Behaviour Therapy may also be effective for Drug-abuse Disorder patients with complex problems attached to the emotional dysregulation who haven't responded to other evidence-based approaches.

DBT And Many Mental Health Problems

(DBT) Dialectical behavioral therapy is a kind of talk treatment that aids you in distinguishing and changing mainly the negative thinking patterns. DBT focuses on individuals with high-risks of behavioral disorders.

It first intended for those with suicidal history and Borderline Personality Disorders. Analysts and researchers say that DBT is useful in treating many mental health problems.

Including The Following:

1. post-traumatic stress disorder (PTSD)
2. anxiety
3. depression
4. Obsessive-compulsive disorder (OCD)
5. Borderline personality disorder (BPD)
6. bipolar

7. autism

8. binge eating disorders.

DBT For Post-traumatic Stress Disorder (PTSD)

(PTSD) Post-traumatic stress disorder is a type of mental and behavior dysfunctional that originates from any apparent danger.

Examples of this can incorporate encountering physical, sexual, or psychological abuse associated with war or battle, prisons, or other criminal acts.

Signs And Symptoms Of PTSD

PTSD can develop at any age, and the indications of the disorder begin after three months of consecutive trauma.

The symptoms of PTSD incorporate the following:

- Encountering the same event; having bad dreams, bad memories, and experiences.
- Avoid any repetitive trauma.

- Avoidance of social meetings.

PTSD is an illness that torments patients since they can't recover from the horrible experience. Instead, the injury threatens them, hurting their wellbeing, connections, way of life, and prosperity. When PTSD goes untreated, patients may go-to medications to cure their signs and symptoms. The mental health of a PTSD can worsen id he is an addict or frequently drinks.

Treatment For PTSD

Dialectical behavior therapy (DBT) is a kind of psychological treatment or that created to treat PTDS, BPD, and other mental health disorders.

DBT focus on changing an individual's thoughts and beliefs about himself, which encourages the changing of habits. The principal focal point of DBT is to assist patients with learning abilities that will diminish emotion dysregulation, senseless behaviors, and other unacceptable ways of dealing with stress.

DBT Helps Treat The Indications Of PTSD By:

Rule out and solve the behavioral variations a person with PTSD feels.

Building up a connection between therapist and patient(s)

The instructing abilities that manage emotions or side effects of PTSD through mindfulness ideas, distress tolerance skills and interpersonal effectiveness skills

DBT assists patients with examining their emotional and mental issues and instructs them to control their conduct. It pushes patients to discover their disturbing experiences and oversee them through the abilities they learn and practice in treatment. DBT shows mindfulness, distress tolerance skill, interpersonal effectiveness, and emotional regulation skills.

DBT For Anxiety

Emotions serve significant roles in our lives. Anxiety directly links emotions such as fear some times it is helpful as they can prevent many life-threatening issues from coming ahead. However, most of the time, emotions like fear emerge when they are not useful or beneficial. These feelings can be hard to change and supervised, further leading to depression anxiety and stress.

DBT works through the way toward learning emotional, cognitive, and intellectual skills, and accordingly applying those abilities to your life experiences. Mostly DBT handles painful and distressing emotions, and it can assist you with improving your strength for an emotional guideline, that is, your capacity to control the feelings you have, when you have them, and experience and express them.

Developing Mindfulness And Distress Tolerance Skills With DBT

Through the DBT skills patient, clint and training groups learn abilities, for example, stress tolerance and mindfulness that guide in acknowledgment of the present time with willingness, instead of battling reality. These procedures could incorporate breathing activities, counting, or holding an ice block to carry mindfulness and acceptance to the present. Events like this urge us to decide to support what's going on at the time. DBT's emotion regulation skills incorporate viewing and representing emotions, alongside an efficient toolkit for adjusting emotions you need to change. These include checking the realities of a circumstance, acting opposite to the active desire of the feeling, and critical thinking to change the incident that is provoking a specific emotional response.

Changing and affecting emotions is a focal objective of DBT. However, before you can find a good pace, it is necessary to comprehend and know where these feelings are coming from and why they emerge. The "understanding and recognizing" chance of DBT is one of the fundamental features that isolate it from customary CBT. DBT is powerful over a scope of psychological wellbeing issues, including mental health issues, because the abilities you learn helps you differentiating facts with emotions, g enabling you to work with and manage emotions viably.

Utilizing DBT To Develop Emotional Skills And Alleviate Anxiety

DBT comprises of a few sections, incorporating individual treatment with a qualified therapist, skilled group coaching, and the specialist's support in a consultation group. Every one of these parts cooperates to guarantee that DBT offers skills that allow you to have self-control over your behavior and emotions If you are experiencing any mental issue, you most likely realize that feeling in charge of yourself is an amazingly important, approving capacity of an individual.

In most situations, regulation of emotions is a skill, and for example, Opposite Action helped some people approach, instead of keep away from circumstances where they felt frightful. Mindfulness skills help many people accept the present situation. Hence they had the option to carry more happiness and importance to their life through trustworthy relationships.

The best part is that what you gain from DBT can be valuable for anybody when you're progressing admirably. DBT offers and shows strong fundamental skills that will stay with us for quite a long time and that we would all be able to implant into our lives.

DBT For Depression

DBT skills groups and training in emergency, along with medicinal administration, brought about critical reductions in sorrow and depression in grown-ups.

The DBT execution in the examination focused on two out of the five treatment DBT treatment modalities: skills group and gathering and instruct them in emergency conditions.

The objectives of these two modalities are to show people new skills and abilities to deal with their feelings. So they could deal with the issues in their lives and to guarantee that they can use those abilities during an emergency.

A significant DBT treatment given to teaching skills. The DBT skills and techniques are intended to help adjust emotions and habits and have four classifications:

1. Skills that develop relational effectiveness in conflict circumstances

2. Techniques and skills that help manage painful feelings

3. Abilities for enduring intense stress

4. Mindfulness skills, intended to assist attention and experience emotions.

DBT For Obsessive-compulsive Disorder (Ocd) DBT for OCD: Acceptance and Non-Judgment

DBT skills are useful for the coping abilities in pain and fear that are associated with daily life. DBT shows that the utilization of cognition like mindfulness, acceptance, and non-judgment can help a lot in many mental health issues, including OCD. Whereas in CBT, the attention is on making and estimating changes in behavior, DBT centered around acceptance and non-judgment. A healthy relationship is primary as individuals figure out how to speak the truth about their behavior and feelings without disgrace or feeling like they have lost. The most important thing is in most people is they need to talk about their efforts, whether they are going in the right direction or not. This progression is regularly vital before they are prepared to make changes.

Studies have discovered that DBT can improve the lives quality and control alongside it lessen sorrow in individuals with personality problem, for example, OCD.

Step By Step Instructions To Apply DBT Skills To OCD

In case you're thinking about how you might have the option to utilized DBT skills with your OCD, here are examples of how these abilities utilized:

Pain and Distress Tolerance: These skills used to either divert or self-calm when confronted with upsetting thoughts or feelings.

Emotional Regulation: By learning techniques and skills to deal with the tension known with obsessions as well as terror, you will understand that your anxiety will decrease with time without yielding to the typical impulse or comfort.

Interpersonal Effectiveness: This arrangement of abilities causes you to deal with your sentiments identified with interactions with others, which may incorporate expecting to look for comfort.

Mindfulness: The ability of mindfulness encourages you to be increasingly present at the moment. Being careful incorporates not holding tight and attaching to upsetting situations, working on being non-judgemental (understanding that your thoughts are neither right nor wrong,) and diverting your thoughts to the present when intervening, dull ideas arise.

DBT For Borderline Personality Disorder.

DBT as a concise treatment intended to serve five functions. Capability improvement depends on the possibility that one of the significant troubles for people with BPD is a deficiency in social skills. Treatment is structured to remediate these deficiencies by helping patients to gain full of emotion, intellectual, physiologic, and social response and their robust execution. DBT looks to achieve this through demonstrating and behavioral reactions of aggressive conduct, psychoeducation, training and feedback, and work assignments. DBT uses motivational improvement to strengthen significant progress and eliminate factors that may hinder successful conduct. The inspirational enhancement is necessary as successful behaviors are regularly blocked by over-learned emotional reactions, ethics, and mental patterns, or on the other hand, environmental hazards that demoralize forceful practice or empower lousy conduct. Strategies to increment inspiration incorporate psychological adjustment, contingency the board, and presentation based procedures.

The objective of enhanced thinking is to guarantee those capable reactions created in treatment moved to patients' lives outside of treatment. Treatment interventions for improving thought incorporate telephone furthermore, E-mail interview, schoolwork assignment, in vivo intervention. The DBT skills and techniques used by professionals may raise the chance of behavioral improvement rather than the risk of self-harm and wrong conduct. Organizing the environment is frequently essential to help the determined conditions that will increase treatment outcomes. The DBT treatment program all in all organized to support treatment progress and marital conduct.

Moreover, DBT may mediate inside the patient's community to additionally encourage the fortification of treatment gains Intercessions for organizing the earth may incorporate associations between the patient and the center director or different overseers, case the board, and family or conjugal intercessions.

DBT tries to treat issues regularly found in professionals treating patients with BPD, for example, burnout, by enhancing expert capacities and inspiration. An isolated expert may experience issues continually confronting tenacious matters, for example, regular emergencies and extreme emotions. Techniques to upgrade specialist inspiration incorporate supervision, proceeding with training, treatment manuals, staff motivating consultation, and a weekly conference group meeting.

The five focuses of DBT tended to all through the different methods of DBT.

DBT For Bipolar

As in standard DBT, we utilized two treatment modalities: skill training (set for individuals family) in which the focus was to show new abilities, and individual treatment, which intends to help the young in applying skills in their everyday lives. Individual therapy sessions organized in standard configuration and target manners and behaviors as per the DBT treatment targets Critical thinking applied, including the lead of behavior chain investigations for targeted issues (e.g., medicine nonadherence) to understand the role of the behavior, discover essential elective solutions, and create procedures for staying away from future behavior issues.

Skills Coaching By Telephone

The professional was accessible to members by pager for in vivo skills training, a vital, but questioning, part of DBT that shows up especially crucial with young clients. Members taught about proper training circumstances. DBT professionals must recognize and observe their own sensible individual limits for calls. Calling the professionals frequently (just as too rarely) is viewed as interfering treatment behavior and is focused on personal sessions. The recurrence of skills training calls not reported in the pilot study.

DBT For Substance Abuse

Dialectical behavior therapy (DBT) is a powerful treatment for addiction treatment. Treatment sessions help an individual beat negative, substance-abuse practices and hurting sentiments. In their place, treatment assist members with making positive thoughts and habits that gather a solid foundation for improving achievement. Addiction regularly powered by self-destructive behaviors and dysfunctional feelings. The physical, mental, and emotional imbalance brought about by overlong medication or alcohol use can irritate these patterns considerably more. This harm can drain an individual's wellbeing, destroy connections, and undermine an individual's employment.

Dialectical behavior therapy stimulates consistency among change and acknowledgment with the goal that an individual is enabled to make strides towards a medication-free life. As treatment advances, an individual figures out how to control desires or longings, manage undesirable feelings, create relapse prevention abilities, and set definite and certifying objectives. Together, these progressions support abstinence and make better brain body-soul balance.

Soon as treatment starts, Dialectical behavior therapy supports total tolerance. For an individual recently in the recovery phase, this can be a scary possibility. Along these lines, DBT separates long term moderation into smaller, and more easy goals to obtain.

The professional may recommend that an individual set a small objective, for example, being calm for 60 minutes, a day, or seven days. When an individual has effectively accomplished this objective, they recharge it and start once more. As an individual keeps on succeeding, they gain stability and draw nearer to long term patience. As treatment advances, DBT focuses on a few practices that improve an individual's possibility of recovery:

- Decreasing or ease withdrawal effects
- Lessening desires and cravings and attractions for relapse

- Expelling social and environmental triggers for drug abuse, for example, people, spots, or occasions.

- Overcoming habits or thoughts that stimulate to take drugs

- Strengthening sound connections, patterns and conditions that help moderation

A primary objective of DBT is to enable an individual to be calm as a "clear mind." In this state, an individual sticks to their recovery objectives while likewise monitoring potential dangers to their calmness. Being careful with a clear head causes an individual to defeat relapse triggers and cope with them.

DBT for Autism

In light of BPD patients, the thoughts move to chemical imbalance specific issues. This attention on balance, mindfulness, nonjudgement, and determined change can give an organized, receptive path for mentally unbalanced people to expose. Acceptance and emotional guideline exercises assist us with creating care intends to use as mediations when our feelings start to get intense—these incorporate things like changing the surrounding which suit you. Our real needs to prevent an emergency, to manage an emergency, and the consideration required after having one

Concentrating on social direction lessens the autistic vulnerability battle within social environments. The breakdown of the limit setting is particularly useful, related to the smart idea. These ideas instruct us to perceive warning behavior and shield ourselves from the individuals who target us. They can likewise assist us with exploring conflicts and keep us from separating individuals who are not abusing. However, they are yet bothering or misunderstanding us.

Developing our emotional and public activities will go far to shield us from self-mischief and suicidality.

DBT For Binge Eating Disorders

Enter dialectical behavior therapy (DBT)— a sort of treatment that consolidates your cognitive behavioral therapy with standards of mindfulness from Zen Buddhism. DBT demonstrated as an active theoretical scheme to encourage the progressions occupant with overeating or binge eating disorder (BED) treatment. Traditional DBT focus on particular social skills for four areas: the emotional guideline, relational effectiveness, stress threshold, and mindfulness. In changing traditional DBT to target binge eating, it likewise incorporates building up an individualized nutriment plan that will bolster their objectives.

The best method to treat binge eating behavior is an idea directly from DBT—it's known as dialectical abstinence, and it indeed finds a good pace of the dilemma inherent in binge eating treatment. One of the central ideas of DBT is finding a dialectical "midway," or a combination, between two restricting thoughts. For individuals with BED, the two curious contradicting views in the argument is

1) You should be only following your diet plan, and that incorporates refraining from particular compelling food

2) Doing that is a complete and definite problem.

From one viewpoint, to make long term settlements, you have to follow a personal diet plan and work your program as a leader with absolute accuracy. However, if it were as simple as "go follow a diet plan accurately," at that point, nobody would be in any food battle predicament. The issue here is that with the individuals who binge eat, the other options for you to being on a plan are genuinely getting the results of the procedure. Or then again, as we officially call it in DBT, the abstinence violation impact: if you have a longstanding battle with a food plan, it's challenging to stick to the program in many ways. You usually don't start it over until you get targeted or been body shamed.

The other thought to diet plan consistency is that the nourishment plan check is inescapable. If you permit yourself not to connect with the diet plans, only shifting turns into the standard, and treatment isn't valid. Four of the riskiest words that notified from clients are "It's No Big Deal" about skipping the diet plan. If these slips are not taken care of, they become relapses, and that would become a longlasting procedure. The issue here is that you don't notice any long term or reasonable change.

DBT discloses to us that the appropriate response doesn't lie exclusively with the imperfection of diet plan and lack of food plan; it lies to be in balance of the therapies. Dialectical abstinence says that breaches will occur AND you can't anticipate them. Argumentative restraint says that we make progress toward recovery/adherence throughout the day consistently. And calls for acknowledgment that fails are an inescapable part of the journey. The DBT system of dialectical abstinence is another perspective on treatment, with specific abilities and skills to explore a person's habits of eating. Emotional guideline techniques help explore those unavoidably ambiguous feelings that give an impact that influences food habits. Interpersonal effectiveness abilities give reliable answers for social difficulties, just as capabilities for discussions to keep in arrangement with characteristics and requirements

DBT: Dialectical Behavior Therapy

The Ultimate 274 Pages Blueprint to Master Dialectical Behaviour Therapy and achieve lifetime Happiness; Never Feel Angry, Sad, Anxious, Depressed, Stressed, and Unhappy Ever Again Part-2

BY

Tom Bhowey

Introduction

If you've ever come across profuse emotions, you know very well what's being talked here. Sometimes, a day comes, and you feel like you hit by a storm. In those moments, a sufferer feels understandably terrifying to feel things because he/she does not want to get swept away by their emotions. The problem is, the more you try to hide or put a stop to it, the more profuse they get. It's necessary to keep in mind that attempting to hide or stop feelings doesn't work.

Dialectical Behavioral Therapy was introduced to the world by Marsha Linehan in 1993. It's an outpatient treatment founded on cognitive-behavioral principles for the patients of parasuicidal behavior in women with Borderline Personality Disorder (BPD). Marsha defines parasuicidal behavior as "any intentional, self-harming behavior with or without suicidal aim, including suicidal attempt and self-damaging behaviors. BPD is a chronic disorder that includes signs such as identity disturbance, unstable relationships, feelings of emptiness, stress, or self-mutilating behaviors.

Dialectical Behaviour Therapy is strongly effective at helping and assisting people in managing profuse emotions. It is supported by research that dialectical behavior therapy makes a person strong at coping distress without losing self-control or behaving in a rubbish manne Many people are suffering from overwhelming emotions generation by generation. It feels like a button is turned to full volume on much of how they feel. When they get annoyed, dizzy, or frightened, it showcases like a strong wave that may sweep them off their feet.

A fair amount of researches advocates that the probability of developing overwhelming emotions may be hardwired from birth. But it can also arise due to childhood neglect. A deeply disturbing or distressing experience during our development can make us vulnerable to depressing emotions. It's a fact that profuse emotions are often deep-rooted into our genetics, but that doesn't mean that its incurable or impossible to treat. This book will address how to control personality disorders, which very possibly be beneficial to you.

In this book, we will go through what is Dialectical Behavior therapy (DBT), how it works, history of DBT, DBT for substance abusers, personality disorders and taking control of personality disorders and much more which will be very beneficial at changing, altering or betterment of your life.

DBT And Relationships

What are the challenges that individuals face with relationships?

Commonly, the problem arises when the people who are in a relationship lose tolerance and are not able to bear each other's personalities. The act of being intolerant may bring about countless discussions and contradictions. Nonetheless, there is a possibility because two individuals with various backgrounds are most likely obliged to have a different point of view. The issue is the point at which the relationship can't figure out how to determine trouble so that there is a breakdown in communication and little a minimal possibility to improve.

Some valuable interpersonal abilities can assist you with managing social conflict, and these begin from Dialectical Behavior Therapy or DBT, supported by the idea of dialectics. A strong point of view includes considering the two sides of a circumstance with the possibility that there would be no similarity between two people having a good relationship. The world is full of changes. In a social setting, this may mean thinking about that "affection" and "hate" can both exist simultaneously, and right now, figure out how to manage stress in the personal situation.

The benefit of doing this is an individual has more decisional stability, which may prompt better decisions. Here's an example to exhibit how dialectical thinking applied in a social issue:

A relationship relates to a tall, green tree. A tree needs a system of healthy roots to feed and strengthen the tree. As the origins of the tree develop, the tree likewise becomes more magnificent, more grounded, and produces fruit. They may even deliver an organic product! Like the tree, your associations with others also have roots. To developing a stable relationship, the sources must be sound. Dialectical behavior therapy (DBT) gives specific abilities to build solid roots and assemble or keep up more advantageous connections. You can easily remember these abilities by their abbreviations: THINK, FAST, GIVE, and DEAR MAN.

Principles Of DBT In Relationships

* DBT in a relationship takes a non-judgemental strategy favoring acceptance and validation of each spouse as well as for himself. A different way of setting this is – producing a mindful recognition of my own life from time to time. And recognition of my life experience of my partner. Along with the information on what is going on for me in this time to time experience.

* DBT in a relationship also converges on what requires change. Moving from negative and refuting responses and comments to one's companion as well himself is made with developing one's emotional self-regulation and stress tolerance.

* Essential to DBT in a relationship is developing the skills to change from emotional dysregulation to improved regulation and efficient communication.

* DBT in a relationship involves developing skills about self-expression – wants, ideas, concerns, cravings – and improving useful problem-solving abilities.

When Do You Need The DBT In A Relationship?

Express anger: complaining your partner about his behavior which will most likely prompt a disturbing and an unpleasant night,

Containing the violence: maintaining a strategic distance from a company and being a friendly partner whether they are having a bad day.

Possibly you have found something comparable, and maybe there were various manners by which you could have reacted to be a helper, companion, child, or parent.
The objectives of DBT's interpersonal effectiveness skills are to assemble and keep up positive connections. These abilities are regularly normal in individuals who have found quality

connections throughout their lives. DBT has analyzed these qualities and framed them into four stable skills. Acing these skills can be useful for anybody, however, particularly for people who have faced trauma or struggle with a relational detachment.

THINK

Think is a more up to date DBT interpersonal skill. DBT Created to lessen negative feelings toward each other. You won't have to utilize this ability in each connection. However, it will be useful when relational problems emerge, and you're feeling annoyed.

Think about the circumstance from the other individual's point of view. Is it true that she is angry, as well? Is it right to say that she sees you as irrational, much the same as you're seeing her odd?

Have empathy — How does it feel like to be the other individual? Let yourself think of her feelings for a minute.

Interpretation — of the other individual's behavior, Consider potential reasons why she did what upset you. Start with odd

motives (to open your personality) and push toward frequently practical goals.
Ideally, these initial three stages will cut your anger level down enough to be increasingly reasonable in your thoughts and activities. That will assist you with the accompanying two steps.

Notice — the other individual. Notice when she is attempting to be benevolent and improve the relationship. Notice that she looks frightened, even though you thought she was distracted. Notice that she grinned at you, although you may not be friends yet. You don't need to take care of business right now, primarily observe the opposite partner for a better understanding of the relationship.

Kindness — in your reaction, this doesn't mean you need to forgive and forget the matter; this implies your words are benevolent. You may state, "What you told me that bothers me, and I believe we can fix this later on. At this moment, I need some space." A benevolent reaction will be better for the long term relationship than verbally abusing and yelling at the partner.

The abbreviation THINK could view as relational stress flexibility skills. When you're in a spot where you feel ready to deal with your feelings toward the other individual, you'll have the option to utilize the following relational effectiveness skills effectively.

Fast

Fast is about your self-respect maintenance during any argument.
You'll need to utilize these skills first in consecutive order, and afterward all together.

Fair — to yourself as well as other people, this act incorporates both your thoughts and your activities. When you're more often fair and reasonable, you are not utilizing emotional or critical ideas or comments, for example, "I'm weak right now" "They're the most terrible situations!" Instead, your thinking lies along the lines of, "What's happening to him, and what's happening for me? or I didn't agree with the majority of what he just stated, however, what were the components of truth?"

(no) Apologies — that doesn't mean you don't apologize when you need to. Saying 'sorry' can be unbelievably amazing when in relationships with someone. Nonetheless, you don't have to apologize when you haven't done anything incorrectly.

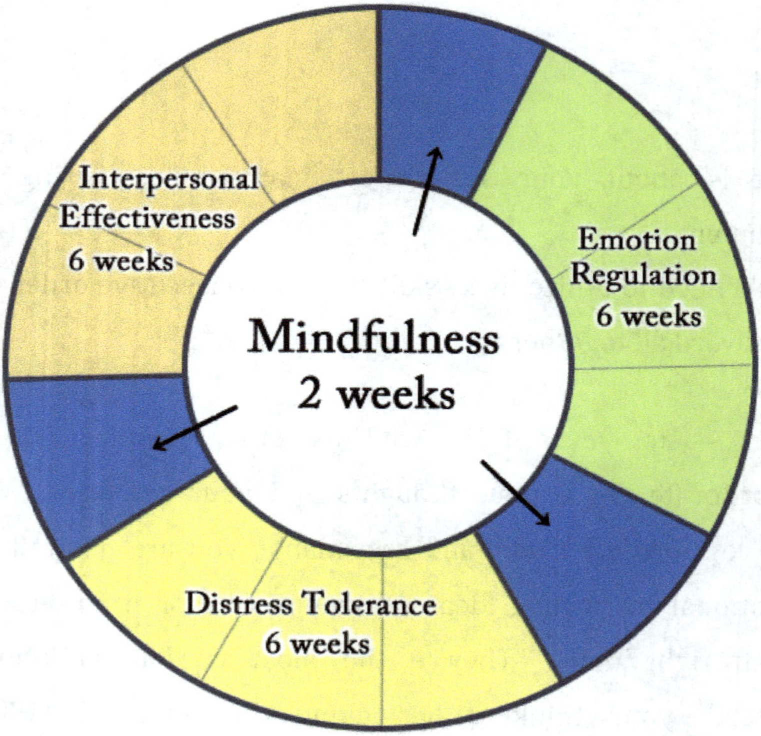

Stick to your qualities — Stand up for what you have faith. In case you don't know what you have confidence in, do some self-assessment to determine your conditions. Speak the truth about what you appreciate. If you state you consider family, however, you maintain a strategic distance from them no matter what, at that point, you do not understand family. You might need to make a review of your present values, and what you trust your characters will be later on depends on it.

Truthful— try to be honest and straightforward with yourself as well as with other people. It is safe to say that you are deceiving the circumstance? Is it fine to say that you are limiting it? Are your words genuine?

Utilizing the four stages of FAST will permit you to keep up your nobility and come out of a circumstance loving yourself, giving little thought to how you feel about the result.

While THINK and FAST utilized in all relational communication, they are particularly useful when there is disagreement in the relationship. For regular relational communication, you can use the skills GIVE and DEAR MAN to grow a healthy relationship.

GIVE

The GIVE skill is valuable in each interpersonal relationship. Regardless of whether it's your first time meeting you or this individual is married to that person for sp long, "GIVE" will assist you with building and keep up positive relationships.

Gentle —be gentle in your methodology. At the point when you're kind, you are aware of the other individual's feelings. Being considerate will assist the individual with whom you're going to feel loved rather than assaulted. Correspondence is, in every case, better when nobody is feeling protective.

Interests— show your full attention to what the other individual is saying. The importance given through words, as well as non-verbal communication in both ways, is an essential part of a relationship. Utilizing words, you can ask the individual inquiries about what she is saying or necessary "uh-huh" "really?" reactions. You can pass on emotions through non-verbal communication by keeping in touch, really tuning in to what she is saying, and making a facial expression.

Validate — Confirm not just that you hear what the other individual is saying, however, that you comprehend it by responding with the feeling back to her. If she is disclosing to you that her friend canceled their get-together for the third time in succession, you may state, "How disappointing! You should feel so sad!"

The easy way — present yourself as being relaxed and friendly all through the relationship. You will generally be more receptive.

Both verbal and nonverbal communication is necessary for the "GIVE" skill. These activities will set you up for effective relational communication in every one of your connections.

DEAR MAN

DEAR MAN is the interpersonal expertise used to request something respectfully and successfully that assembles and keeps up a relationship- - regardless of whether you get what you are asking.

Describe — the circumstance in a fundamental manner. if you need to go out to see the films with your friends, you could quickly imitate the situation by saying, "My friends are going to see the new comic book motion picture this end of the week."

Express — what you might want. "I might want to go out to see the film with my friends."

Assert — why this is imperative to you in a manner that is informed and not persuasive. "I haven't had the option to invest a lot of time with them since track season began, so it would be extremely significant if I could spend time with my friends."

Reinforce — when you get what you requested. "I guarantee I'll have my room clean, and my work is complete before I leave for the motion picture with my friends."

Mindful — Stay at that time. Don't stress yourself for the past or future, for example, what your friends will say if you can't go. Just live the moment.

Appear Confident — would you say you are terrified to approach your manager for a raise? She doesn't have to realize that. Surely approach the circumstance. It would be best if you built some confidence in you.

Negotiate — when it doesn't appear that you will get the outcome you were needing, be adaptable. Try to find out the happiness in what you have in a relationship.

Emotional Regulation Skills

Emotional regulation skills assist you in recognizing the role emotions perform in your decision-making power and regularly on your actions. Determining ways to control emotions can have a definite impact on how you develop or adapt to circumstances so that the outcome can be more beneficial. It is likely to learn new ideas to answer to situations and learn to new prospects. Even with painful trauma and abandonment practices, these skills can improve perspectives and emotions that can lead to enhanced feelings and experiences.

- Learn to recognize and identify emotions without judging

- Recognize barriers to changing emotions, exercise redirecting ideas

- Decrease vulnerability to a sensitive mind, self-care methods
- Develop positive, passionate events
- Enhance mindfulness to familiar emotions
- Take the opposite action
- Utilize distress tolerance skills or practice mindfulness exercises.
- Deep breathing

Practical Interpersonal skills trained in DBT can improve the likelihood of favorable results in relationships and assist you in maintaining happy, healthy relationships for the long-term. When used, useful DBT skills can allow you to grow relationships on the grounds of respect, honor, compassion, and attachment. If you hold this skill in mind, you would not be having any trouble keeping and managing relationships.

A quick guide to DBT

Dialectical Behavior Therapy (DBT)

Dialectical behavior therapy provides patients with new skills to manage harmful or painful emotions and minimize disputes in relationships. The main focus of DBT is to provide therapeutic skills in four main areas. First, call mindfulness, this therapy focuses on improving and changing the attention of an individual's ability and to make them present in the current moment. Second, which is distress tolerance, it helps the people to understand negative emotions, rather than escaping from it. The third one Is Emotion regulator. This therapy helps a person to cover strategies and manage intense emotions that are causing on one's life. The fourth one is interpersonal effectiveness, which is consists of techniques that allow a person to communicate or talk to others in such a way that shows confidence, self-respect, and give strength to relationships.

When is DBT Used?

It is originally developed to treat a personality disorder. However, research shows that it is beneficial for people who are suffering from bulimia, bipolar disorder, depression, binge-eating, post-traumatic-stress disorder, and substance abuse. Dialectical behavior therapy skills are for those who want to tolerate distress, improve their ability to regulate emotions and negative emotions, and want to be mindful and present at the moment.

What to Expect from DBT?

Usually, DBT treatment consists of individual therapy or group therapy. The individual therapy sessions are one on one sessions with a trained therapist, who ensure that all the therapeutic basics and needs are being addressed. The benefit of individual therapy is that the therapist helps the patient to stay motivated, address obstacles that will arise during DBT, and apply the DBT skills in daily life.

While DBT skills group team learn from each other and practice the techniques and apply the skills together, group members share their experiences and provide support to each other. This mutual support helps patients to come out of a depressing situation quickly. The team of DBT skills runs by one trained therapist who teaches skills and exercises. Sometimes, the trainer assigns them homework, such as mindfulness exercises. The approximate duration of each group is two hours, and this group generally meets once in a week for six months. Depending on the needs of group members, the group duration can be shorter or longer.

DBT is possible in many ways. For example, some complete individual sessions without attending the group sessions while others may choose group therapies without meeting the therapist in one on one.

How DBT Works

This treatment is developed by Marsha Linehan, Ph.D., in the 1989s. The purpose of this treatment is to cure people with borderline personality problems. Those who are diagnosed with borderline personality disorder (BPD) sometimes experience intense negative thoughts that are hard to manage. These uncontrollable and intense negative emotions are commonly experienced when the patient is interacting with friends, others, romantic partners, or family members. People with this problem often experience high disputes and mismanagement in their relationship.

The name DBT is influenced by the thoughtful touch of dialectics: to balance opposites. The therapist continuously works with the individual to find different ways to hold two opposite perspectives at once. The aim is to promote balance and avoid the 'all or nothing' styles.

Why DBT is Effective for treating Borderline Personality Disorder (BPD)

DBT is best for those people who have complex mental disorders that are too difficult to treat. The DBT treatment is effective in borderline personality disorder because it has a problem-solving and proactive approach that teaches the skills needed to improve relationships, to control intense emotions, reduce self-destructive behavior, and manage distress.

These skills for effective treatment of BPD take time in learning. Learning different components of therapy, including individual therapy, group therapy, and phone calls, takes over one year or more time.

Main components of DBT

Support-oriented: This helps the people to know their strengths and build their power so that the patient can feel better about their life.

Cognitive-based: DBT helps a patient to identify beliefs, thoughts, and assumptions that make life harder and depressed: "I have to be right all the time." "If I get angry, I am a terrible person," and it helps people to make life more bearable. Like everyone gets angry, it's normal.

Collaborative: collaboration required constant relationships between clients and counselors (therapist).In DBT, people want to work on their problems with their therapist, and the therapist treats them the same as they want. DBT assigns homework to complete and to learn new ways of interacting with people and practicing new skills. These skills are critical parts of DBT that are taught in weekly meetings, and review it with time to time. The individual therapist helps the patient to learn and master DBT skills.

Generally, DBT has mainly two concept

1. Individual weekly psychotherapy sessions: The main emphasis of this session is problem-solving—the problems that arise in the patient's life and how he/she deal with the problem. Suicidal behaviors and self-injuries are the number one priority in individual weekly sessions. The therapist sees the response of patients during therapies. Quality of life and working toward improving life experience may also be discussed. In DBT, the individual sessions also focus on dealing with post-traumatic stress and help patients to enhance their own self-respect and self-image. Between sessions, the therapist teaches adaptive behaviors. The emphasis is to teach people how to manage or deal with

emotional trauma instead of reducing or taking them out of crises. Telephone contact with a therapist is part of DBT procedures. During individual sessions of therapy, the therapist and client work together to learn and improve the necessary social skills.

2. Weekly group therapy sessions: in general, its ½ to 2 hours of sessions. It is led by a trained therapist. In this group therapy session, people learn the skills of different modules. Like emotion

regulation, mindfulness, interpersonal effectiveness, and distress tolerance/ reality acceptance skills

4 Modules of Dialectical Behavior Therapy

Interpersonal Effectiveness

The interpersonal response patterns of how you interact with people in surrounding and in your personal relationships that are taught in dialectical behavior therapies. These skills also include effective procedures for asking what one needs, how to confidently say 'no,' and learn to deal with inevitable interpersonal disputes.

People with borderline personality often possess excellent interpersonal skills. Some may be able to describe useful behavioral sequences when talks about another person encountering a difficult situation but may be totally incapable of carrying out a similar set of behaviors or actions when analyzing or interpreting their own personal situation.

This session focuses on situations where the aim is to change something (e.g., when you request someone to do something) or to try to resist when someone else is trying to change (like saying no).the interpersonal effectiveness skills are taught I order to maximize the chances that a person's goal in a specific circumstances will be met.

Distress Tolerance

Many approaches in mental health treatment focus on changing the distressing events and situations. They pay little attention to accept, to find meaning in life, and tolerate distress.
Generally, this task is tackled by spiritual and religious leaders and communities. Dialectical behavior therapy focuses on learning to take pain skillfully.

Distress tolerance skills add up a natural development from mindfulness skills. They have to accept, in a nonjudgmental and non-evaluative fashion, both their own self and the current situation. Although the attitude recommended, here is a nonjudgmental one.

This behavior is concerned with surviving and tolerating crises and accepting life as it is. Therapists taught us four sets of survival strategies: self-soothing, improving the moment, distracting, and thinking of pros and cons.

Emotion Regulation

People with a borderline personality disorder or who may be suicidal usually are emotionally intense and easily altered. They get angry frequently. They are intensely frustrated, anxious, and depressed. This suggests that people struggling with these concerns might benefit from help to regulate their emotions.

DBT for emotion regulation includes:

- Learn to identify and label emotions accurately

- To identify obstacles and changing emotions

- to reduce "emotional mind" vulnerability

- taking opposite actions
- to increase positive emotional events
- to increase mindfulness to current emotions
- Mindfulness
- the core and essential part of all skills are mindfulness
- Observing, describing, and participation are the core mindfulness skills. They answer the questions," what I am doing to practice the core mindfulness skills?"
- One-mindfully and effectively non-judgmentally are the "how" skills and answering the questions.

What to Look for in a DBT Therapist

DBT assumes that productive or successful treatment is group skills training. They pay so much attention to the behavior and attention of the providers working with clients, as they pay attention to the client's experiences and responses. Thus, it's also crucial in DBT to treat the provider very well, and therapists should practice the skills themselves as well. They must know the basic techniques of behavior therapy DBT treatment strategies. Search for someone who is professional and has specialized training experience in DBT. It is essential to find therapists with whom you are comfortable, and you understand his/her strategies.

Some other disorders that can be treated with DBT

Skills that people learn in DBT are sometimes useful in treating other forms of emotional challenges and mental illness. One of the skills that are taught in DBT is mindfulness. This skill helps people focus on the present moment, decrease negative emotions, and improve well-being.

Some other skills used in DBT and mindfulness practice may be useful in treating:

Anxiety: To reduce intense emotions and modify behaviors, DBT teaches the skills needed to tolerate emotional intensity.

Depression: DBT teaches people to know what they might do to feel better and to recognize how to take charge of their lives.

Addiction and eating disorder: addiction to sex, shopping, shopping, food, and gambling are ways to manage overwhelming or painful feelings, so the skills that are used in

DBT are useful in regulating and reducing those emotional reactions.

Bipolar disorder: People with anxiety, those with bipolar disorder can benefit from learning the skills in DBT to bear the emotions that go with mood swings and behavior changes need to reduce emotional reactions.
If you want to treat different mental and emotional disorders, mental health professionals and therapists can guide each patient to the type of therapy that is likely to be most useful in their individual cases.

For the treatment of different mental and emotional disorders, doctors or mental health professionals can guide each person to the form of therapy that is likely to be most effective in their individual case. DBT is an innovative approach to the treatment of BPD, and it is found to be useful for other mental challenges as well.

Is DBT is Right Choice for You?

The majority of the research, till now, has focused on the effectiveness of DBT for people with borderline personality disorder (BPD), and different types of dangerous thoughts like suicidal, self-harm, substance use disorders, and post-traumatic stress disorder. DBT also works in a variety of mental health conditions. Like:

- Bipolar disorder
- Bulimia
- Generalized anxiety disorder
- Post-traumatic stress disorder
- Substance use disorder
- Suicidal and self-harming behavior
- Generalized anxiety disorder
- Major depressive disorder(chronic depression, treatment-resistant major depression)

? Research shows that DBT is useful for age, sexual orientation, race/ethnicity, and sex.

□

? The best way to know if DBT is the right choice for you is to talk with a mental health professional or psychiatrist, who will judge your symptoms, your treatment history, and will provide you therapy goals to determine the best next steps.

□

? **Dialectical thinking:**

□

? Dialectical thinking allows a person that two ideas can be right. In reality, there are always many ways

□

? To see and handle the situation. Life consists of both comfortable and uncomfortable situations, so to believe this process and keep your mind open provides you the opportunity to accept the challenges of life. Understanding the four core principles of DBT challenges people to avoid black and white thinking and find out alternatives ways of situation. This expands a person's understanding of the world, and this thinking allows them to tolerate, accept, and cope with the way the world is.

□

The treatment shows many pieces of evidence that DBT is useful in treating suicidal ideation, mood disorder, and change in behavioral patterns such as substance abuse, and self-harm. In DBT treatment, the client and the therapist work together and agree on the process of change-oriented strategies, balance, and synthesize the philosophical dialectical process of antithesis and hypothesis, which is followed by synthesis. This approach was developed by Marsha Linehan to help people increase their emotional and cognitive regulation by learning about the triggers that lead to reactive states and helping to assess which coping skills to apply in the sequence of events, thoughts, feelings, and behaviors to help avoid undesired reactions. Because dialectical behavior therapy has been demonstrated to be useful for treating a variety of severe problems across patient populations, the demand for DBT training of mental health professionals has substantially increased.

Advantages of dialectical behavior therapy:

The following are some of the benefits of DBT:

- Decreasing high risk suicidal and self-harming behavior.
- Decreasing therapy interfering behaviors
- For reducing behaviors that interfere with the quality of life.
- Learning and mastering behavior skills for mood-independent life choices

- Decreasing symptoms related to trauma, stress, anxiety, and depression

- Enhancing and sustaining self-respect

- Assistance with goal setting to create a life worth living.

⍰

By focusing on facts rather than emotions or value judgments such as right/wrong or fair/unfair, DBT residents enhance their abilities to respond positively and productively, without descending into self-blame or other destructive thoughts and behaviors.

DETAIL AND EXPLANATION:

Capacity enhancement: DBT allows for developing new existing skills. In DBT treatment, therapists teach four skills.

- Mindfulness
- Emotions regulation

- Interpersonal effectiveness

- Distress tolerance

Generalization: The therapists use different methods to encourage people to transfer their skills in them. They also learn how to apply what they learn at school, at home, at work, and in the community.

In DBT therapies, a patient can learn how to use or apply the skills they have learned in schools or at home, at work, and in community. For instance, the therapist may ask the patient to talk about the conflict with his or her partner. Here the patient can use emotion regulation therapy during or after discussion **Motivational enhancement**: DBT uses specific behavioral treatment procedures to minimize the dangerous behaviors that might affect the quality of life. For example, therapists sessions can be adapted to deal with the most critical issues first.

Capacity and motivational improvement of therapists: people who prefer doing DBT or someone else told them to do it often experience severe, chronic, and intense mental issues. Therapists who do therapies are under great supervision to prevent things like burnout and traumatization. For instance, to provide and receive support treatment, teams often hold a meeting with therapists.

The structure of the environment: one goal of therapy is to ensure positive and adaptive behaviors in every kind of situation. For instance, if one person is participating in multiple treatment programs with one agency or organization, the therapist must make sure each program is set up to strengthen all the positive skills and behaviors. DBT has many standard forms of therapies like individual therapy, phone coaching, group training, and therapist consultation team. Those who take the therapy sessions with groups attend the sessions once a week. The group aims to help those who are in the treatment process. And they can learn behavioral skills through group work and with homework assignments. Tasks that people practice aim to gain expertise in day-to-day life.

Phone coaching is an important part of DBT. Phone coaching helps people to reach out to the therapists when they face a challenging situation between sessions.

Patients and therapists recreated a pattern of reinforcement in which good work was obstructed, and avoidance was encouraged. When therapists drive them for change, the patients react in anger. When therapists allow a subject change, the patients responded with helpful and positive feedback. This loop seemed to trick both patients and therapists into thinking they were on the right track. Due to the strength of crisis-related situations, therapists spent a great deal of time to address safety concerns, such as hostility, self-injuries, suicidal thoughts or gestures, and threats towards the therapist. Often, little time was left to teach coping skills or address behavioral functioning. Secondary analyses indicated that DBT was associated with significantly higher rates of clinically significant change, defined as the absence of any self-harm.

Youths in the DBT group attended significantly more treatment sessions than did youths in the IGST group and were significantly more likely to complete treatment.

Although the results of pattern-mixture models found no evidence of an informative attrition mechanism, we cannot rule out the possibility that differential treatment exposure is a mechanism that leads to the DBT outcomes.

Stronger DBT treatment retention is, however, an important finding given prior research that found difficulties with treatment engagement and adherence among suicidal and self-harming youths.

The DBT has now changed into a normal kind of cognitive-behavioral therapy. When the individual is experiencing DBT, they can imagine contributing in three therapeutic settings: A classroom is a place where a person is trained behavioral skills by doing different homework projects and role-playing new habits of interrelating with different people. Normally the class meets for two to three hours once a week. The people attend that class. They do take an interest in different activities. In DBT therapy, you will work on four specific areas of functioning. These include decreasing some behaviors and increasing others: The single person therapy with a skilled expert where those educated behavioral skills are modified to the person's personal life tests. Running concomitantly with the classroom work, individual therapy meetings usually last for 60 minutes in seven days. The Phone education in which a person can call their counselor in among meetings to obtain supervision on coping with a difficult at-the-moment state in their life.

While the individually therapeutic setting has its personal set structure and goalmouths, the next features of DBT are originated in group skills training, individual psychotherapy, and phone coaching stands for Dialectical Behavior Therapy. It was developed by Dr. Marsha Linehan, investigated heavily, and then available in 1993. This is possible because when you will join any of the services on the Adult Outpatient Unit while you will be for your broadcast. There are some medicine management services and group therapy, and also short-term individual therapy. The person will need to go through the consumption to partake in these services. Feel free to let the intake clinician know that you are on the waitlist for DBT. The Family and couples' sessions fundamentally are not usually a part of adult DBT treatment. Though, if the individual person and the therapist trust any of the next is happening, a family couple's session may ultimately be shown: The person will be asked for the next session meanwhile they want to discuss something with your family member important other and would like the separate therapist there as a trainer. There is a tragedy exploding in the Family that is receiving in the way of development family member significant other is doing something that is strengthening a behavior that you and the therapist are directing, and the counselor has faith in that you have not yet erudite the essential skills to achieve the situation on your own. There is a forthcoming risk to safety, and you have asked for your family noteworthy other to be communicated.

For the reason that any medical treatment is the careful ancillary treatment to DBT, you may keep sighted by your outside psychiatrist. Though, there are a few things to consider when doing so: DBT uses a technique called discussion to the client, which means that you will supervise discussing any subjects that come up with your psychiatrist. Your individual therapist will not be talking to the psychiatrist on your behalf under most circumstances. If you have any talk therapy with your counselor.This is need to stop when you join our DBT program. Doings with your counselor are to emphasize only on subjects connected to medicine and medical circumstances. Not at all. Most of the clients who come to DBT have sole or numerous shocks. Though, in DBT, we trust that if the person does not have the services to deal efficiently in their daily lives, they surely do not have the skills essential to work through trauma efficiently. As a result, trauma treatment is optional and shown after the client's complete skills exercise and are no longer showing self-harm and unhappy behaviors. Ways to distract: The person should do something, whatever to get your mind off your emotions. They should Play video games and straighten your closet, and they should get involved in some exercise. They should always make sure that the action they choose doesn't strengthen your aching emotion. They should not play a violent video game when they are previously feeling annoyed. Instead, they should also visit their favorite coffee shop and get a mocha or whatsoever hot drink you love. They can also support a friend, buy a homeless person a meal or

helper. They should do very nice things for others not only takes your mind off your doubts for the instant but can also have the additional advantage of making sense of sense or purpose in your life. They should read, watch, or listen to something that will bring on other emotions: To do this, they should figure out what emotion they are feeling. Then they should read a book, watch a movie, or they can listen to their favorite music that suggests a feeling that is different than the one your sensation. When a person is feeling sad, they should listen to upbeat music. If you're annoyed, they should watch a funniness. When the person is feeling desperate, read about people who conserved in difficult times. This is one of the great to use when the person is in public, and they need a private way to sidetrack yourself. When the person Count 20 things, they see around you that are blue, rerun the different words in a song in your mind, count to 1000. Let an ice cube dissolve in your hand, and they should take a hot bath or suck on a slice of lemon juice. Basically, the significance of using distraction is not to misuse it. The Sidetrack is a very real short-term solution that will also help you evade doing something you'll later regret, but it's not an answer to solving life's problems. In order to solve life's problems, they will have to attraction to other DBT services when you're in your astute mind. The person should know Distracting works since it would help make a little interplanetary among you and whatever is hurtful you. An additional advantage is that occasionally off-putting also helps to change your painful emotions. We need that the person should be willing to work

on dipping and eventually stopping the use of illegal materials in order to be in the program. At the same time, contingent on the giving problems, material use may not be the top priority at the beginning of therapy unless it somehow causes and relates to behaviors like suicide and self-harm. When customers have done with their first year of treatment and are still consuming ingredients. The person will be essential to decide to work on discontinuing the material use if they are to endure in our program. This is for the reason that in the second year of action, clients will need to be livelier in discovering their own intelligent mind and adaptable their emotions, somewhat that is nearly unbearable when under the effect of substances. The Family and couples' sessions basically are not generally a part of adult DBT handling. But, when the separate therapist trusts any of the next is happening, a family couple's session may eventually be conducted: You will be asked for the session since they really want to deliberate something from your family member significant other and would like the individual therapist there as a trainer. Here is a disaster erupting in the Family that is getting in the way of progress family person other is doing something that is strengthening a performance that you and the therapist are directing. So the counselor trusts that you have learned the necessary helps to achieve the state on your own. So there is an imminent risk to safety, and you have asked for your family/significant other to be contacted. The DPT We have together male and female customers, and also we have male and female therapists in our program.

Disadvantages of DBT:

Many kinds of research suggest that DBT is an effective treatment for mental health problems. But DBT has some limitations. All the research that yet done on DBT shows the effectiveness of small sizes on the specific sectors of the mental health population. Some experts argue, more research should be done to determine if DBT works well for different or more complex mental health concerns.

DBT uses a detailed manual and solid training to implement. In many research studies where DBT found to be successful, the DBT therapists were doctor-level therapists or higher. The developer, Marsha Linehan, trained most. The therapy does not necessarily indicate a weakness in the version of the treatment itself but emphasizes the in-depth amount of training required to deliver the facilities as designed. Increasing the availability of comprehensive training is useful for the community mental health organizations. Some DBT research trails last up to a year.

But, it's not yet examined whether the therapeutic gains last beyond the post-treatment follow up Interviews. Due to the persistent nature of the conditions treated, the field of DBT could benefit from more research by measuring treatment gains.

Strategy, A person, should know:

Strategies in DBT refer to the role and focus of the therapist, as well as to a coordinated set of procedures that function to achieve specific treatment goals.

Although DBT strategies usually consist of several steps, the use of a strategy does not necessarily require the application of every level.

It is considerably more important than the therapist apply the intent of the strategy than that he or she should inflexibly lead the client through a series of prescribed maneuvers.

Dialectical Strategies

Dialectical strategies permeate the entire therapy, and their use provides the rationale for adding the term "dialectical" to the title of the therapy.

There are three types of dialectical strategies: those having to do with how the therapist structures interactions; those on how the therapist defines and teaches skillful behaviors; and certain specific strategies used during the conduct of treatment.

Balancing Strategies:

"Dialectical strategies" in the most general sense of the term have to do with how the therapist balances the dialectical tensions within the therapy relationship. As noted earlier, the fundamental dialectic therapy within any psychotherapy, including that with a client who has BPD, is that between acceptances of what is and efforts to change what is. The DBT positions one of constant attention to combining acceptance and change, flexibility and stability, nurturing and challenging, and a focus on capabilities and a focus on limitations and deficits. The main goal is to find out the odds in both the client and the therapist and to provide conditions for the union. The presumption is that change may facilitate by emphasizing acceptance, and acceptance by emphasizing change. The emphasis upon opposites sometimes takes place over time (i.e., over the whole of an interaction). Rather than simultaneously or in each part of an interaction. Although many psychotherapies, including cognitive and behavioral treatments, attend to these issues of balance, placing the concept of stability at the center of the treatment ensures that the therapist remains attentive to its importance.

Three primary characteristics are needed to maintain a dialectical stance in the therapeutic relationship: movement, speed, and flow. Movement refers to acting with certainty, strength, and total commitment on the part of the therapist If the therapist only moves halfheartedly, the client will only move halfheartedly.

Speed is of the essence and entails keeping the therapy moving so that it does not become rigid or stuck. Finally, flow refers to being mindful of the moment-to-moment unfolding of a session and responding smoothly and with apparent effortlessness.

Teaching Dialectical Behavior Patterns:

Dialectical thinking emphasizes throughout the entire treatment. Not only does the therapist maintain a dialectical stance in his or her treatment of the client, but he or she also focuses on teaching and modeling dialectical thinking to the client.

The therapist helps the client move from an "either-or" position to a "both-and" position, without invalidating the first idea or its polarity when asserting the second. Behavioral extremes and rigidity— whether cognitive, emotional/overtly behavioral —are signals that synthesis has not been achieved; thus, they can be considered no dialectical. Instead, a "middle path" similar to that advocated in Buddhism is recommended and modeled.

The essential thing in following the path to Enlightenment is to avoid being caught in any extreme and always follow the Middle Way. Specific Dialectical Strategies:

There are eight specific dialectical treatment strategies:

- entering and using paradox
- Extending
- Playing the devil's advocate
- Using metaphor
- Making lemonade out of lemons (by turning negatives thoughts into positives).
- Assessing dialectically by asking the question always, "What is being left out here?"
- Activating the client's "wise mind,"
- Allowing natural change

ENTERING THE PARADOX:

Entering the paradox is a powerful technique because it contains the element of surprise. The therapist presents the contradictions without explaining it and highlights the paradoxical contradictions within the behavior, the therapeutic process, and reality in general. The essence of the strategy is the therapist's refusal to step in with rational explanation; the client's attempts at logic are met with silence, a question, or a story designed to shed a small amount of light on the puzzle to be solved. The client is propelled to achieve understanding, to move toward a synthesis of the polarities, and to resolve the dilemma himself or herself.

Linehan has highlighted many typical paradoxes and their corresponding dialectical tensions encountered throughout therapy. Clients are free to choose their behavior but cannot stay in treatment if they do not work at changing their behavior.

They are taught to achieve greater independence by becoming more skilled at asking for help from others. Clients have a right to kill themselves, but if they ever convince the therapist that suicide is imminent, they may be locked up.

Patients are not responsible for being the way they are, but they are responsible for what they become. In highlighting these paradoxical realities, both client and therapist struggle with confronting and letting go of rigid patterns of thought, emotion, and behavior, so that more spontaneous and flexible patterns may emerge.

USING METAPHOR: PARABLE, MYTH, ANALOGY, AND STORYTELLING:

The use of metaphor, stories, parables, and myth is significant in DBT and provides an alternative means of teaching dialectical thinking. Stories are usually more interesting, are easier to remember, and encourage the search for other meanings of events under scrutiny.

Additionally, metaphors allow clients to distance themselves from the problem being discussed and can, therefore, be less threatenin

In general, the idea of metaphor is to take something the client does understand and use it as an analogy for something the client does not understand.

Used creatively, metaphors aid understanding, suggest solutions to problems, and reframe the issues of both clients and the therapeutic process. Furthermore, metaphors and stories can be developed by both therapist and client, taking turns throughout a session or treatment.

When the therapist and client relationships to a metaphor, it can be a powerful tool to use throughout the treatment, reminding the client what he or she is working. For example, changing behavior by learning new skills can be compared to building a new hiking trail in the woods.

At first, the current trail is defined and easy to navigate; however, it always leads to a dead-end (old dysfunctional behavior). To build a new path (skillful behaviors), the hiker must repeatedly go through a unique, undefined area until it becomes worn in. This takes time, and the hiker moves slowly and deliberately clearing away the brush. Additionally, while the new path is developing, the old road is gradually becoming grown over.

This story can be returned to throughout treatment; each time, the client begins to struggle between trying new skills and returning to old dysfunctional behavior.

PLAYING DEVIL'S ADVOCATE:

The devil's advocate technique is quite similar to the argumentative approach used in rational–emotive and cognitive restructuring therapies as a method of addressing a client's dysfunctional beliefs or problematic rules.

With this strategy, the therapist presents a propositional statement that is an extreme version of one of the client's own dysfunctional beliefs, then plays the role of devil's advocate to counter the client's attempts to disprove the outrageous statement or rule.

For example, a patient may think, "Because I'm overweight, I'd be better off dying." The therapist argues in favor of the dysfunctional belief, perhaps by suggesting that because this is true for the client, it must be valid for others as well; hence, all overweight people would be better off dead.

The therapist may continue along these lines: "And since the definition of what constitutes being overweight varies so much among individuals, there must be an awful lot of people who would be considered overweight by someone. That must mean they'd all be better off dead!" Or "Gosh, I'm about 5 pounds overweight. I guess that means I'd be better off dead, too."
Any reservations the client proposes can be countered by further exaggeration until the self-defeating nature of the belief becomes apparent. The devil's advocate technique is often used in the first several sessions to elicit a firm commitment from the client and in commitment sessions with new therapists joining the DBT team.

The therapist argues to the client that since the therapy will be painful and difficult, it is not clear how making such a commitment (and therefore being accepted into treatment) could be a good idea. This often affects patients to move to take opposite positions for the change of therapeutic favor. If you want to utilize this technique successfully, it is essential that the therapist's argument seems reasonable enough to invite counterargument by the client and that the delivery is made with a straight face in an offbeat but straightforward manner.

MINDFULNESS AND WHAT IT IS?

Mindfulness is also known as meditation; it's a valuable skill that has been taught for thousands of years in many of the world's religions, including Christianity, Judaism, and Buddhism.

So, what mindfulness is? Mindfulness is the capability to be aware of your thoughts, physical sensations, emotions, bodily sensations, and actions—in the present moment—without judging or criticizing yourself or your experience.

WHY ARE MINDFULNESS SKILLS IMPORTANT?

The mindfulness skills will help you focus on one thing at a time in a present moment, and by doing this, you can better control your overwhelming emotions. Mindfulness will help you learn and separate judgmental or negative thoughts from your experiences. These critical thoughts often fuel your overwhelming emotions. In mindfulness, a therapy called a wise mind is a beneficial skill in dialectical behavior therapy.

USE SELF-ENCOURAGING DEALING THOUGHTS:

We face many distressing times in life when we all need to listen to some encouraging or motivational words to keep us motivated and to help us endure the pain that we're suffering. However, there are many times like these when you are also alone, and you need to encourage yourself to stay strong, active, and healthy. Often, this can be done with self-encouraging coping thoughts.

List of Coping Thoughts:

- "My life will change with time."
- "I can be anxious and still deal with the situation."
- "I've been through a lot of challenging experiences, but I passed and survived."
- "My feelings are making me uncomfortable right now, but I can accept them."
- I'm powerful to handle what's happening right now."
- "Dealing with my fear is an opportunity for me."

- “I can take all the time I need to let go and relax.”
- “I have passed through many other same situations, and I will pass this too.”
- “My fear/sadness/anxiety won’t kill me; I know it's not feeling good right now.”
- “Its only feelings which well go away.”

EXTENDING:

Extending is a term that is borrowed from aikido, a Japanese form of self-defense. In the DBT context, extending occurs when the aikido students wait for a tough or challenging movement to reach their completion, then the students continue the movement’s endpoint little further than the natural occurrence.

In DBT, extending occurs when the therapist takes the severity or gravity of what the client is communicating more seriously than the client intends. This strategy is the emotional equivalent of the devil’s advocate strategy. It is particularly useful when the client is threatening dire consequences of an event or problem to induce a change in the environment. Take the interaction with the following client, who threatens suicide if an extra appointment time for the next day is not scheduled. The following interchange between therapist and client occurs after attempts to find a mutually acceptable time have failed.

Example:

CLIENT: I've got to see you tomorrow, or I'm sure I will end up killing myself. I can't keep it together by myself any longer.

THERAPIST: Hmm, I didn't realize you were so upset! We've got to do something immediately if you are so distressed that you might kill yourself. What about hospitalization? Maybe that is needed. CLIENT: I'm not going to the hospital! Why won't

you give me an appointment? THERAPIST: How can we discuss such a mundane topic as session scheduling when your life is in danger? How are you planning to kill yourself?

CLIENT: You know-how. Why can't you cancel someone or move an appointment around? You could put an appointment with one of your students off until another time. I can't stand it anymore! THERAPIST: I'm concerned about you. Do you think I should call an aid car? The aspect of the communication that the therapist takes seriously (suicide as a possible consequence of not getting an appointment) is not the aspect (needing an extra appointment the next day) that the client wants to be taken seriously. The therapist takes the consequences seriously and extends the seriousness even further.

Core Strategies

Validation

Together dialectical strategies and problem-solving strategies are the main types of DBT and form an essential part of the treatment. Validation strategies are the clearest acceptance strategies, whereas problem-solving strategies are the most evident change strategies.

Both strategies (Validation and problem-solving) uses with every interaction with clients, although the related frequencies of both depend on the particular client, their current situation, and the vulnerabilities of the client. However, throughout an entire session, there should be an overall balance between acceptance and change strategies. Many treatment impasses are due to an imbalance of one type of strategy over the other.

We discuss validation strategies in this section and problem-solving strategies in the next. Clients with BPD present themselves clinically as individuals in extreme emotional pain. They plead, and at times demand that their therapists do something to change this state of affairs.

It is very tempting to focus the energy of therapy on changing the client by modifying irrational thoughts, assumptions, or schemas, critiquing interpersonal behaviors or motives contributing to interpersonal problems, giving medication to change abnormal biology, reducing emotional over-reactivity and intensity, and so on.

In many respects, this focus recapitulates the invalidating environment by confirming the client's worst fears: The client is the problem and indeed cannot trust his or her reactions to events. Mistrust and invalidation of how one responds to events, however, are incredibly aversive and can elicit intense fear, anger, and shame, or a combination of all three.

Thus, the entire focus of change-based therapy can be aversive because the focus by necessity contributes to and elicits self-invalidation. However, focus as a whole of acceptance-based treatment can also be invalidated when it appears to the client that the therapist does not take his or her problems seriously.

Therefore, once again, a dialectical stance focuses on a balance between the two poles. Validation means "the action of validating or making valid . . . a strengthening, reinforcement, confirming, and establishing or ratifying." It also encompasses activities such as corroborating, substantiating verifying, and authenticating.

To communicate that a response is valid is to say that it is "well-grounded or justifiable: being at once relevant and meaningful . . . logically correct. Appropriate to the end in view [or effective] . . .

having such force as to compel serious attention and [usually] acceptance."

These are precisely the meanings associated with the term when used in the context of psychotherapy in DBT: The essence of Validation is this: The therapist communicates to the client that her responses make sense and are understandable within her current life context or situation. The therapist actively accepts the client and delivers this acceptance to the client.

The therapist takes the client's responses seriously and does not discount or trivialize them. Validation strategies require the therapist to search for, recognize, and reflect the client the validity inherent in her response to events. With unruly children, parents have to catch them while they're right to reinforce their behavior; similarly, the therapist has to uncover the validity within the client's response, sometimes amplify it, and then enhance it. Two things are essential to note here. First, Validation means the acknowledgment of that which is valid.

It does not mean "making" valid. Nor does it mean validating that which is invalid. The therapist observes, experiences, and affirms, but he or she does not create validity.

Second, "valid" and "scientific" are not synonyms. Science may be one way to determine what valid, logical, sound in principle is, and generally accepted as the authority or normative knowledge. However, an authentic experience or apprehension of private events (at least, when similar to the same experiences of others or when in accord with other, more observable facts) is also a basis for claiming validity. Validation can be considered at any of six levels.

Each level is correspondingly more complete than the previous one, and each level depends on one or more of the earlier levels. These are the definitions of DBT and are required in every interaction with the client. These levels are described most fully in Linehan, and the following definitions are taken from her discussion.

LISTENING AND OBSERVING (V1)

Level 1 validation requires listening to and observing what the client is saying, feeling, and doing, as well as a corresponding active effort to understand what is being said and found. The essence of this step is that the therapist is staying awake and interested in the client, paying attention to what the client says and does in the current moment. The therapist notices the nuances of response in the interaction.

Validation at Level 1 communicates that the client per se, as well as the client's presence, words, and responses in the session, have "such force as to compel serious attention and [usually] acceptance."

ACCURATE REFLECTION (V2)

The second level of Validation is the accurate reflection back to the client of his or her feelings, thoughts, assumptions, and behaviors. The therapist conveys an understanding of the client by hearing what the client has said and seeing what the client does and how he or she responds. Validation at Level 2 sanctions, empowers or authenticates that the individual is who he or she actually is.

ARTICULATING THE UNVERBALIZED (V3):

In Level 3 of Validation, the therapist communicates an understanding of aspects of the client's experience and response to events that have not been observed directly by the client. The therapist "mind-reads" the reason for the client's behavior and figures out how the client feels and what he or she is wishing for, thinking, or doing just by knowing what has happened to the client. The therapist can link precipitating events and behavior without being given any information about the response.

The therapist articulates emotions and meanings the client has not expressed.

VALIDATING IN TERMS OF PAST LEARNING OR BIOLOGICAL DYSFUNCTION (V4):

In Level 4, the behavior is validated in terms of its causes. Validation here is based on the notion that all behavior is caused by events occurring in time; thus, in principle, it is understandable. The therapist justifies the client's behavior by showing that past events cause it.

Even though the information may not be available to determine all the important causes, the client's feelings, thoughts, and actions make perfect sense in the context of the client's current experience, physiology, and life to date.

At a minimum, what "is" can always be justified in terms of sufficient causes; that is, what is "should be" in that whatever was necessary for it to occur had to have happened.

VALIDATION IN TERMS OF PRESENT CONTEXT OR NORMATIVE FUNCTIONING (V5):

At Level 5, the therapist communicates that behavior is justifiable, reasonable, well-grounded, meaningful, and efficient in terms of current events, normative biological functioning, and the client's ultimate life goals. The therapist looks for and reflects the wisdom or validity of the client's response and communicates that the reaction is understandable.

The therapist finds the relevant facts in the current environment that support the client's behavior. The therapists are not blinded by the dysfunctionality of some of the client's response patterns to those aspects of a response pattern that may be either reasonable or appropriate to the context. Thus, the therapist searches the client's responses for their inherent accuracy or appropriateness or reasonableness, also commenting on the inherent dysfunctionality of much of the reaction, if necessary.

RADICAL GENUINENESS (V6):

In Level 6, the task is to recognize the person as he or she is, seeing and responding to the strengths and capacities of the client while keeping a firm empathic understanding of his or her actual difficulties and incapacities. The therapist believes the client and his or her ability to change and move toward ultimate life goals just as the therapist may believe in a friend or family member.

The client is responded to as a person of equal status due to some respect. Val dating at the highest level is the Validation of the individual as "is." The therapist sees more than the role, more than a "client" or "disorder." Level 6 validation is the opposite of treating the client in a condescending manner or as overly fragile.

It is responding to the individual as capable of effective and reasonable behavior rather than assuming that he or she has a disability.

Where as Levels 1–5 represent sequential steps invalidation of a kind, Level 6 represents the change in both level and type. Cheerleading strategies constitute another form of Validation and are the principal strategies for combating the active passivity and tendencies to hopelessness in clients with BPD.

In cheerleading, therapists communicate the belief that clients are doing their best and validate clients' ability to eventually overcome their difficulties (a type of Validation that, if not handled carefully, can simultaneously invalidate clients' perceptions of their helplessness). Also, therapists express a belief in the therapy relationship, offer reassurance, and highlight any evidence of improvement.

Within DBT, cheerleading use is in every therapeutic interaction. Although active cheerleading by therapists should be reduced as clients learn to trust and to validate themselves, cheerleading strategies always remain an essential ingredient of a strong therapeutic alliance.
Finally, functional Validation, another form of Validation that is used regularly in DBT, is a form of nonverbal or behavioral validation that, at times, maybe more effective than verbal Validation. For example, a therapist drops a 50-pound block on

the client's foot. It would be a 50-pound block on the client's foot.

It should be invalidated for the therapist to respond verbally, saying, "Wow, I can see that hurts! You must be in a lot of pain." Functional Validation would entail the therapist removing the block from the client's foot.

DBT Vs. CBT

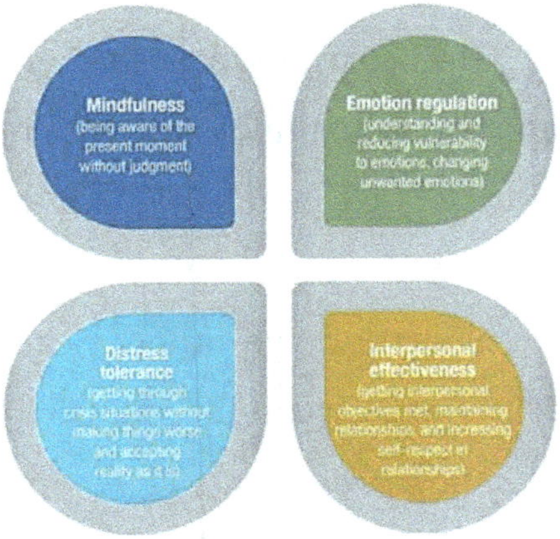

Psychotherapy is one of the most effective treatment ways on the market for a variety of mental sicknesses. One amongst the foremost common sorts of medical aid is named psychological feature activity medical aid (CBT). Conjointly known as to speak medical aid, CBT focuses on talking concerning your issues to assist you in framing your thoughts otherwise. If square measure Like negative thoughts is perpetually up to the mark, I am a failure. I can't do something right. Nobody can like me if they see United Nations agency I actually am." CBT will assist you to use logic and reason to flip the script and be up to the mark of your thoughts rather than permitting your thoughts to regulate you. However, commonplace CBT isn't effective in treating all mental sicknesses. Another common form of medical aid is named Dialectical Behavior Therapy (DBT). DBT could be a lot of specific type of CBT that focuses on serving to those that tend to own extreme emotional reactions act with the surroundings around them in an exceedingly less emotional, healthier method With such similar names, square measure CBT and DBT that totally different from one another, and might victimization one have advantages over victimization the other? Scan on to be told concerning the variations between CBT vs. DBT and the way to work out that one can best assist you.

CBT could be a catch-all phrase for therapies that share common characteristics. DBT could be a form of CBT, alongside many different varieties. Therapists United Nations agency apply CBT typically apply to speak medical aid that depends on many guiding options.

Those options include:

Treats Emotional Response: Supported the concept that our thoughts influence our feelings; therefore, dynamic the method we expect concerning and react to things can facilitate the United States of America to feel higher. Limited to a selected amount of Time: most patients can get treatment for an amount of your time then begin to use CBT methods on their own while not vital support from a psychological state skilled. If mood or behavior issues persist, purchasers might then attain a special form of medical aid to handle a selected trauma or different issue that continues to cause pain or be a barrier to healthy living. Having an honest Therapist-Patient Relationship: CBT works best once the patient looks like they will trust their expert. As a result of the non-public nature of medical aid, patients ought to search out somebody they respect and feel comfy. Relies on knowledge and Rationale: CBT encourages patients to use logic and reason to assist direct; however, they reply to things rather than rental emotions do all the driving.

Uses Structure to Guide Treatment: Therapists have a selected reason for the techniques and ways they carry up in every session. They use the client's goals to work out that CBT ideas are most helpful to them and tailor each consequently. While DBT could be a form of CBT, it's tailored towards serving individuals acknowledge the pain and discomfort they feel; however they still feel safe and "ok" within the moment and authorized to settle on healthy behaviors rather than impulsive or harmful actions whereas some stress is placed on handling thoughts, the patient's square measure educated to spot triggers outside of themselves and match those triggers with a healthy cope mechanism or response.

CBT Vs. DBT for Treating sure sickness:

Not all mental sicknesses reply to treatment within the same method. A medical aid technique that works well for depression and anxiety will exacerbate ingestion disorders or temperament disorders.

CBT has been shown to be implausibly effective once treating depression and is a lot of seemingly to form depression go in remission than different sorts of medical aid. This methodology of medical aid has conjointly been established helpful in treating anxiety because it provides patients management over their recovery. CBT has conjointly been shown to assist with the psychoneurotic compulsive disorder (OCD), phobias, anxiety disorder, post-traumatic. Stress disorder and sleeping problems.

DBT was created to assist those diagnosed with a borderline psychological disorder. DBT focuses on serving individuals amendment their behavior patterns, as hostile attempting to suppose or speak through the problems they're combating. This kind of CBT helps people who have developed patterns of intense emotional reactions and impulsive behaviors in response to what patients describe as overwhelming feelings of pain and rejection of the sensation of walking through a world full of knives. DBT typically is that the handiest medical aid for people who struggle with self-harm behaviors like cutting and chronic, dangerous thinking. Sexual trauma survivors conjointly respond well to DBT techniques.

BT focuses on reasoning and explanation, as most ordinarily found in stoic philosophy and also the pedagogy. The pedagogy uses important thinking to question assumptions in situ. This works well for people who suffer from anxiety and depression because it helps them to check their issues from

a lot of logical purpose of reading. For instance, purchasers United Nations agency struggle with feelings of failure and inadequacy square measure asked to seem at the facts once they indeed been roaring at accomplishing a goal? Square measures there people friends, family, or co-workers United

Nations agency may provide proof of the client's success in numerous situations? United Nations agency or what square measure they victimization as a measure for success?

DBT depends heavily on heedfulness skills utilized in Buddhism and Zen practices. DBT teaches patients to use specific heedfulness techniques to be told to measure with pain within the world and settle for; however, things square measure rather than suffering by attempting to alter them. The distinction in Treatment ways:

- CBT focuses on; however, your thoughts, feelings, and behavior influence one another. Whereas DBT will work on this stuff, stress is given a lot of towards regulating emotions, being conscious, and learning to accept pain.

- CBT seeks to administer patients the flexibility to acknowledge once their thoughts would possibly become hard and offer them techniques to send those thoughts

- DBT helps patients realize ways in which to accept themselves, feel safe, and manage their emotions to assist in regulating doubtless harmful or harmful behaviors.

- Clients United Nations agency have interaction in DBT medical aid participate in DBT skills coaching sessions that square measure generally educated in an exceedingly cluster setting in four modules.

 Most patients conjointly meet weekly with a DBT expert or DBT coach and receive DBT phone coaching jobs once they need to facilitate the foremost. Sometimes, once patient's square measure able to use DBT skills to manage their emotions, apply heedfulness, and improve relationships with others, they're able to transition to a lot of commonplace CBT teams to handle specific negative thought patterns or continual harmful behaviors.

□

⍰ CBT and DBT are each common forms of cognitive-behavioral medical care, conjointly referred to as speak medical care, that are supported cognitive-behavioral techniques. They're each meant to assist in healing the people with psychological state disorders, especially people who struggle with suicidal behaviors. While they're supported identical techniques, you'll be inquisitive what very makes them totally different and that one could be higher for your kid. This text can address what every sort of medical care is, what makes them totally different from each other, and why we tend to suggest Sunrise as a DBT treatment center for young ladies scuffling with psychological state disorders.

□

⍰ Cognitive psychotherapy, or CBT, was developed within the Nineteen Sixties by Dr. Aaron T. Beck. In his search to higher perceive people who struggled with depression, he found that there was an associate degree underlying issue that stemmed from what he referred to as 'automatic thoughts.'

⍰ These were negative thoughts and beliefs that shoppers had regarding themselves, the world, and, therefore, the future. These automatic thoughts, or thought distortions, are what Dr. motion wished to pinpoint with patients so they may work on cognitively restructuring their unsuccessful thoughts to positive and healthy thoughts.

□

⍰ In order to know CBT, it's smart to be at home with the thought that our thoughts verify our feelings that, in result, verify our behavior. Therefore by ever-changing our thoughts, we tend to are ready to ultimately modification our feelings and behaviors, which might dramatically improve our lives. CBT is primarily centered on the assumption that the manner we predict is what causes North American nation pain, and if we make the modification, it'll considerably improve our overall well-being. As a result of CBT heavily depends on speak medical care with the patient and expert, there has to be an honest relationship established, so the shopper feels trust with their expert. The shopper conjointly has to be willing to try to work needed to spot the negative thought patterns and to require to try to the work to very them. Dialectical psychotherapy, or DBT, was developed by Marsha Lineman within the late Nineteen Seventies. Exploitation CBT techniques in her medical care, she began to notice that some issues were arising. Patients would get annoyed and quit medical care as a result of they weren't feeling valid. They felt just like the emotions they were experiencing were being reduced.

As a result, they didn't have a robust relationship with their expert. Lineman realized that acceptance and validation are a robust part of the healing method; therefore, she determined to make on CBT principles and created what's currently referred to as DBT, a mindfulness-based psychological feature medical care.

DBT relies on CBT; however, together with modification, it adds another part that Lineman felt was missing: acceptance and validation, whereas DBT was at first created to assist folks with a selected kind of disorder.

Borderline psychological disorder(BPD) its currently to with success treat several temperament disorders and psychological state challenges. The two key differentiators between DBT and CBT are acceptance and validation.

Acceptance: DBT needs the patient to accept the sentiments they need and to acknowledge them as real and valid. By inceptive that it makes the modification, they have to try to appear supportable. Validation: once a patient receives validation from their expert that the emotions feeling are real, it helps build a trust therein relationship. Having that trust, along with your expert, is crucial if the shopper goes to create any changes in his or her life. By having an honest balance of acceptance and alteration, DBT permits the expert and shopper to take care of an honest balance inside medical care. Instead of specializing in modification solely, validation was introduced not to downplay the emotions shoppers were feeling.

The shopper associates degreed expert work along at finding the final word balance of acceptance and alter, so neither one is too way on an extreme facet. Keeping this balance inside medical care sessions is essential to assist the shopper to come back to on a path to emotional and mental healing. [DBT] skills enable you to reply in ways in which assist you in coping and handle distress instead of responding in negative or suicidal ways that. DBT is separated into five talent teams, with the primary 2 (mindfulness and distress tolerance) specializing in acceptance and, therefore, the third and fourth (emotion regulation and social effectiveness) specializing in modification. The fifth talent (walking the center path) focuses on finding that balance of acceptance and alteration. These skills enable you to reply in ways in which assist you in coping and handle distress instead of responding in negative or suicidal ways that. This can be why DBT is improbably palmy in managing people who are dangerous or people who have an inclination to self-harm as a result of they learn cope skills that employment during a style of things. Another side of DBT that sets it with the exception of CBT is that the DBT cluster sessions. These facilitate the shopper to possess an extra medical care session that has other UN agency is learning DBT. It provides a grade of treatment for a person that goes on the far side simply ancient shopper and expert sessions. Having the ability to figure with other UN agency are learning identical skills provides a way of happiness and security that helps eliminate the isolation that CBT will bring.

Dialectical behavior modification (DBT) provides shoppers with new skills to manage painful emotions and reduce conflict in relationships. DBT specifically focuses on providing therapeutic skills in four key areas. First, heedfulness focuses on a personality's ability to accept and be a gift within the current moment. Second, distress tolerance is meshed toward increasing a person's tolerance of negative feeling, instead of making an attempt to flee from it. Third, feeling regulation covers methods to manage and alter intense emotions that square measure is inflicting issues during a person's life. Fourth, social effectiveness consists of techniques that enable someone to speak with others during an approach that's assertive, maintain self-esteem, and strengthens relationships.

DBT was originally developed to treat borderline disturbance. However, analysis shows that DBT has additionally been used with success to treat folks experiencing depression, bulimia, binge-eating, manic depression, post-traumatic-stress disorder, and abuse.

DBT skills square measure thought to possess the potential of serving to people who want to enhance their ability to manage emotions, tolerate distress and negative feeling, be aware and gift within the given moment, and communicate and move effectively with others. DBT treatment usually consists of individual medical care sessions and DBT skills teams.

Individual medical care sessions incorporate one-on-one contact with a trained healer, making certain that each one therapeutic wants square measure being addressed. The individual healer can facilitate the patient to keep intended, apply the DBT skills at intervals standard of living, and address obstacles that may arise over the course of treatment.

DBT skills cluster participants learn and apply skills aboard others. Members of the cluster square measure inspired to share their experiences and supply mutual support. Teams measure junction rectifier by one trained healer teaching skills and leading exercises. The cluster members square measure then assigned schoolwork, like active heedfulness exercises. Every cluster session lasts roughly 2 hours, and teams usually meet weekly for six months. Teams may be shorter or longer counting on the requirements of the cluster members

DBT may be delivered by therapists in many ways. As an example, some folks complete the one-on-one medical care sessions while not attending the weekly skills cluster. Others would possibly opt for the cluster while not regular one-on-one sessions. DBT could be a cognitive-behavioral treatment developed by Marsha Linehan, Ph.D. within the Nineteen Eighties, to treat folks with borderline disturbance.

Those diagnosed with BPD usually expertise extraordinarily intense negative emotions that square measure tough to manage. These intense and apparently uncontrollable negative emotions square measure usually knowledgeable once the individual is interacting with other friends, romantic partners, relations. Folks with borderline usually expertise a good deal of conflict in their relationships. As its name suggests, DBT is influenced by the philosophical perspective of dialectics: equalization opposites. The healer systematically works with the individual to search out ways in which to carry two apparently opposite views quickly, promoting balance and avoiding black and white the all-or-nothing varieties of thinking. In the commission of this balance, DBT promotes a both-and instead of AN either-or outlook. The dialectic at the guts of DBT is acceptance and alter.

What seems for during a dialectical Behavior healer. DBT assumes that effective treatment, as well as cluster skills coaching, should pay the maximum amount of attention to the behavior and skill of suppliers operating with shoppers because it will respond to clients' behavior and skill. Thus, the treatment of the suppliers is a very important part of any DBT program, and therapists ought to apply the talents themselves. They have to grasp basic behavior modification techniques and

DBT treatment methods. Seek for a mental state skilled with specialized coaching and skill in DBT.

The Linehan Board of Certification, a non-profit organization, has developed certification standards for clinicians. Additionally, it's necessary to search out a healer with whom you are feeling comfy operating.

The goal of DBT is to assist you in learning to manage your difficult emotions by letting yourself experience, recognize, and accept them. Then as you learn to accept and regulate your emotions, you furthermore may become more ready to change your harmful behavior. to assist you in achieving this, DBT therapists use a balance of acceptance and alter techniques. "I had bounced in and out of psychological state services for an extended time, and the zip had helped, my condition had just worsened. Then I started DBT. Now I do know what helps me, and I even have strategies when life is hard. Not everything is obvious sailing, but when things go a touch wrong, I recover instead of spiraling's focuses on helping you to vary unhelpful ways of thinking and behaving.

DBT also helps you to vary unhelpful behaviors, but it differs from CBT there in it also focuses on accepting who you're at an equivalent time. "I had bounced in and out of psychological state services for an extended time, and the zip had helped, my condition had just worsened. Then I started DBT. Now I do know what helps me, and I even have strategies when life is hard. Not everything is obvious sailing, but when things go a touch wrong, I recover instead of spiraling."

DBT (Dialectical Behavior Therapy) Treatment

In DBT, the present-day quantity of disordered conduct determines what remedy tasks are relevant and feasible. For example, what is applicable and feasible for a homeless consumer with out of manipulate heroin use who has angrily blown out of a couple of methadone remedy programs, and who has recently attempted suicide, is exceptional than what is applicable and viable for a nurse, also hooked on opiates, who prevented a suspended

interventions for addiction will be the same, the first character desires more comprehensive help. Treating a number of her behaviors (e.g., suicide attempts) will take priority over treating others. Multiple problems (e.g., drug abuse, homelessness, out-of-manipulate anger) may additionally want to be solved simultaneously.

In a common-sense way, DBT's level model of treatment prioritizes the issues that must be addressed at a particular factor in therapy according to the chance they pose to the purchaser's reasonable quality of lifestyles. The first level of remedy with all DBT clients is pretreatment, followed via one to Four subsequent stages. The range of subsequent stages relies upon the quantity of behaving.

In the pretreatment degree as with other CBT approaches, the purchaser and the therapist explicitly and collaboratively conform to the critical dreams and techniques of treatment. While it's far no longer vital to have a written contract, it is important to have a mutual verbal dedication to treatment agreements. Specific agreements might also vary with the aid of setting and clients' issues; however, the consumer might encompass agreeing to work on the Stage 1 remedy targets for a specified duration of remedy and attend all scheduled sessions, pay fees, and the like. For the therapist, they might include agreeing to provide high-quality treatment possible (including increasing his or Her own talents as needed), to abide by ethical principles, and to participate in the consultation. Such agreements need to be in place earlier than starting formal remedies.

Because DBT calls for voluntary in place of coerced consent, both the consumer and the therapist Must have the choice of committing to DBT over some different Non-DBT option. So, for example, in a forensic unit or whilst a client, is legally mandated to treatment, he or she is Now not considered to have entered DBT till a taken into consideration verbal commitment is obtained. In pretreatment, once the therapist commits to the customer, the concern is to reap engagement in therapy. Stage 1 of DBT is for the most intense stage of the disorder. Stage 1 of remedy objectives Behaviors had to gain seasonable existence expectancy management of actions and sufficient connection to treatment and behavioral abilities to acquire these goals.

If you want to attain these dreams, treatment time is allocated to present priority to goals inside the following order of importance:

(1)suicidal/homicidal or different imminently life-threatening behavior. (2) therapy-interfering conduct by way of the therapist or the patron. (3) Conduct that critically compromises the purchaser's high-quality of existence (e.g., Axis I issues as well as serious problems with relationships, the

felony system, employment/school, illness, and housing); And (4) Deficits in behavioral competencies needed to make lifestyle changes. DBT assumes that positive deficits are particularly relevant to BPD and provide training to help clients (5) alter emotions; (6) Tolerate distress;
(7) Respond skillfully to interpersonal situations;
(8) Observe, describe, and participate without judging, with recognition and focusing on Effectiveness; and (9) Control their own conduct with strategies aside from self-punishment. Regulation capabilities decreasing labile have an effect on and immoderate anger and distress tolerance supporting to lessen impulsive behaviors, suicide threats, and intentional self-injury. It's vital to notice that DBT actively targets remedy-interfering behaviors of both the customer and the Therapist, viewing it as second only to lifestyles-threatening conduct. In different words, customer behaviors that interfere with receiving therapy along with not attending, noncollaboration, and noncompliance, or that push therapist limits or

lessen his or her motivation to treat the purchaser is viewed on an equal footing as behaviors of the therapist that unbalance therapy along with being extraordinarily accepting or extraordinarily change-focused, too flexible or Too rigid, too nurturing or too withholding, and so on. Specific targets are mutually diagnosed after which are monitored and provide the principle schedule for character remedy sessions alongside assisting the client reach man or woman dreams.

DBT, it's far crucial to speak that the dreams of remedy are not truly to suppress excessive dysfunctional behavior; however, instead of building a lifestyle that any reasonable character would don't forget well worth living.

Many clients who are not out of control nevertheless experience first-rate emotional pain due to both posttraumatic strain responses or different painful emotional reviews that go away them alienated or remoted from meaningful connections to different humans.

They suffer lives of quiet desperation, wherever emotional expertise is either too Intense (although behavioral management is maintained) or the person is numbed.

Therefore, with these shoppers, the Stage a pair of goals of medical care e to possess no traumatizing emotional experience and affiliation to the surroundings.

In Stage three the shopper synthesizes what has been learned, will increase his or her self-regard and an imperishable sense of affiliation, and Works toward breakdown issues in living.

Targets here are self-regard, mastery, self-efficacy, a way of morality, and appropriate quality of life.

It focuses on the sense of wholeness that several people expertise, even when issues in living are basically resolved.

For many, Stage four goals fall outside the realm of Traditional medical care and at intervals, a religious apply that offers rise to the capability for freedom, joy, or religious fulfillment.

Although the stages of medical care are conferred linearly, progress is commonly not linear and The stages overlap. it's not uncommon to come back to discussions like those of pretreatment To regain commitment to the treatment goals or ways. The transition from Stage one to Stage a pair of is additionally troublesome for several, as a result of exposure work will cause intense, painful emotions and ensuant behavioral decontrol. Like alternative trauma approaches (cf. Follette & Razak, 2006), DBT encourages the acquisition of skills to a sufficient level that one contains a reasonable quality of life/stability of behavioral management before systematic exposure to the cues that are related to past traumas.

The rareness of Stage one behaviors as Well, because the speed of reregulation (rather than the presence of anyone instance of behavior) defines the variations between stages. Readiness for Stage a pair of work is individual.

In general, the shopper is prepared for transition once he or she is not any longer participating in severe dysfunctional behavior will maintain a powerful medical care relationship and has incontestable to his or her own and also the therapist's satisfaction with the power to deal with cues that are using to depart drawback behavior.

Stage three is commonly a review of similar problems from a distinct viewpoint. The level of disorder and stages of treatment have implications for service delivery.
Many clinics have completely different levels of care contingent on the severity of behavioral Decontrol. What's needed is to possess reinforcers (e.g., a lot of and a lot of in-depth services) Available contingent progress instead of the continuation of nonadaptive behavior.

For example, if it's the case that somebody will solely get individual medical care by being fully out of management or that shoppers lose access to individual therapists as shortly as they're Out of crisis, then the contingencies favored a lack of progress and continued crises. As mentioned earlier, responsibility for treating specific targets is appointed to modes. For example, the individual clinical psychologist is appointed the role of treatment designing, ensuring that progress is created on all DBT targets, serving to integrate alternative modes of Therapy, consulting to the shopper on effective behaviors with alternative suppliers, and management of crises and dangerous behaviors. this enables the first therapist who is often the one who best is aware of the client's capabilities to teach, to strengthen, and to generalize the shopper's new responses to crises while not reinforcing client dysfunctional Behavior. This additionally prevents multiple various treatment plans from being run right away.

The skills trainer's role is to confirm that the shopper acquires new skills. to maximize learning and keep roles from conflicting, he or she solely minimally target behaviors that interfere with skills coaching (e.g., dissociating in a cluster, coming back late), referring the shopper Back to the first individual healer to figure on the majority of these issues.

Similarly, in unsafe and alternative crises, the abilities trainer refers to the shopper back to the individual healer, when conducting a requisite suicide risk assessment and providing the intervention. It is needed to urge the shopper in-tuned with the first healer.

Dialectical ways

A number of ways square measure enclosed in DBT that serve the operate of keeping polarized Positions from remaining polarized. The primary of those is those core ways square measure accustomed balance acceptance and alter. For instance, DBT needs an expert to own a balanced communication vogue. On the acceptance aspect, the expert employs a responsive style during which the client's agenda is taken seriously and responded to instead of interpreted for its latent, which means. For instance, if a consumer asks one thing personally concerning the expert, the expert is a lot of seemingly to use self-disclosure, heat engagement, and genuineness either to answer the question or to matter-of-factly decline to answer based mostly on his or her limits. However, this vogue alone or associate degree imbalance toward this vogue will cause impasse.

When the glum consumer World Health Organization has told the identical story of grievance, again and again, features an expert World Health Organization merely paraphrases within the same monotone because the consumer the chance is that the client's mood can keep identical or worsen. The client's mood can keep identical or worsen.

Consequently, reciprocal communication is balanced by irreverence that jolts the person, of course, to permit the consumer to resume the The therapeutic task at hand. for instance, the expert, would possibly use associate degree unorthodox, offbeat manner. The expert, World Health Organization, had been as engaged because the consumer in an exceeding power struggle suddenly shifts tone and laughs, "You know, this moment is not as black and white as I had hoped. Equally, the expert could plunge in wherever angels concern to tread. Example, he would possibly say matter of fatly to the girl whose major precipitant to dangerous crises are that the threat of losing her husband, "Look, cutting yourself and exploit blood all over the lavatory is destroying any hope of getting a true relationship together with your husband." Or the expert would possibly advise a replacement consumer, "Given that you've raped 2 of your three last therapists let's kick off with what crystal rectifier up to it and the way it's not planning to happen with Maine. I'm planning to be of no use to you if I'm frightened of you." mistreatment associate degree irreverent type of communication includes employing a resistance tone, mistreatment humor or unconventional phrasing, oscillatory intensity, or every now and then expressing state or impotence in the face of the client's issues.

Another way that DBT balances acceptance and alter is just in case management ways. people World Health Organization meet criteria for BPD usually have multiple treatment suppliers and Consequently, a variety of ways are developed to assist the client-therapist dyad in managing the relationships with different clinicians and members of the family. DBT is weighted toward a consultation to the client strategy that emphasizes amendment. The DBT therapist consults with the consumer concerning the way to handle relationships with different treatment providers and members of the family, instead of consulting with different treatment suppliers and Family members concerning the way to upset the consumer. So, for instance, this implies that the The therapist doesn't meet with different professionals concerning the consumer; however, rather than the consumer is a gift at treatment designing conferences. Instead of meeting with another supplier while not the consumer gift, a phone call might be regular throughout a personal session. If the expert needs to meet while not the client gift for a few sensible reasons the speech communication is shared with the consumer or mentioned earlier, this same principle holds for

conversations with the client's family.

Even in an exceeding crisis, the spirit of consulting to the consumer is maintained whenever attainable. The consumer shows up within the hospital room, and also the sorting nurse or resident on decision contacts the expert to raise the expert what he or she would really like done, the DBT experts initially raise to talk with the consumer so as to debate with

the consumer however going in the hospital will and doesn't coincide with the client's semi-permanent goals and their Agreed-upon treatment arrange. The expert would possibly then coach the consumer on the way to act skillfully with the hospital room (ER) employees or have the consumer communicate the commit to The ER employees and so merely ensure that with the employees, if that's needed for credibleness. If the hospital employees were involved concerning suicide risk and were reluctant to unharness the person, the DBT expert wouldn't "tell" the hospital employees to unharness the consumer, but instead would possibly coach the consumer on what was required to decrease the legitimate worries of ER employees. The DBT expert can intervene within the setting on the client's behalf once the Short-term gain is definitely worth the semi-permanent loss in learning for The expert could decision a client's bluff or use extending bluff or use extending, for example, once a consumer on associate degree inmate unit threatens suicide in associate degree angry or blasé manner, the expert would possibly say, "Listen, this can be very serious. We should go straight away and place you on the line of sight observation and acquire you into a suicide robe.

Informed by dialectical philosophy, the expert and also the treatment team assume that their case formulations square measure partial and thus move to assess what's overlooked once There is associate degree impasse (dialectical assessment). The expert could read a discouraging event as a chance to follow distress tolerance (making fruit drink out of lemons) or allowing instead of preventing natural amendment (such as a bunch leader exploit and being It replaced), knowing that this, too, is a chance to follow acceptance of reality.

DBT therapist and the questions/answer class

The DBT has now changed into a typical kind of cognitive-behavioral therapy. When the individual is experiencing DBT, they can imagine contributing in three therapeutic settings: A classroom is a place where a person is trained behavioral skills by doing different homework projects and role-playing new habits of interrelating with different people. Usually, the class meets for two to three hours once a week. The people attend that class. They do take an interest in various activities.

The single person therapy with a skilled expert where those educated behavioral skills are modified to the person's life tests. Running concomitantly with the classroom work, individual therapy meetings usually last for 60 minutes in seven days.

The Phone education in which a person can call their counselor in among meetings to obtain supervision on coping with a problematic at-the-moment state in their life. While the individually therapeutic setting has its set structure and goalmouths, the next features of DBT are originated in group skills training, individual psychotherapy, and phone coaching **Reduce or eliminate pain**. Therapeutic movements and manual therapy methods such as joint and soft tissue enlistment or actions, including ultrasound, taping, and electrical motivation, can help release discomfort and reinstate muscle and the joint role to decrease pain. These types of treatments can also stop pain from returning.

Avoid surgery. If corporeal therapy helps you remove the pain or heal from a wound, the operation may not be needed. And even if surgery is obligatory, you may advantage of pre-surgery and physical therapy. When the person is going into an operation stronger and in improved shape, they will recover faster later in many cases. Also, by evading surgery, health care costs are reduced.

Improve mobility. If you're having trouble standing, walking, or moving, no matter your age, physical therapy can provide assistance. Widening and strengthening movements help restore your ability to move. Physical therapists can properly fit persons with a cane, props, and any other assistive expedient, and measure for orthotic medicine. Modifying the separate care plan, whatsoever activity that is vital to an individual's life, can be skillful and modified to safeguard the best presentation and safety.

Support Attitude: The person will be stimulated to know your positive fortes and qualities and develop and use them. They would feel very positive.

Behavioural: The person will learn to examine any problematic or unhelpful behavior designs and substitute them with the fit and real ones. It will help them out.

The Cognitive: The person will focus on moving thoughts or politics and conduct or actions that are not real or helpful.

Skill sets: The person will learn new assistance to improve their capabilities in different ways.

Acceptance and change: You'll learn plans to accept and tolerate your life, emotions, and yourself as well as skills to help you make positive changes in your behaviors and interactions with others.

Collaboration: The person will learn to connect efficiently and work together as a team therapist, group therapist, a psychiatrist. They would feel positive.

.

DBT distraction techniques

The DBT distract skill is different

It's not mindlessly when you are checking your phone. It's not obsessively rerunning a fight with your life partner in your skull while circumnavigating rush hour traffic with your radio blaring. It's focused. If you are selecting to do somewhat else instead of doing those types of things, your feelings are telling you to do when you are in tension. Just Because acting on your emotions when you're super animated usually only boomerangs.

Occasionally not fully feeling our emotions is a very good thing for the person. Likewise, when the person has the tempting need to start weeping at a work meeting when you feel disapproved by your manager or boss. It's perhaps wise not to let the emotional state out.

The DBT distract skill will help the person focus their attention away, so they would not lose it publicly.

- The skills which are extremely useful when the person

- When the person is very speechless with the emotions. It will help them.

- You have needed to do things you will later regret badly.
- The person will feel an irresistible earnestness to fix a problem right now

- When a person is in the sentiment mind, the person act needs can be very substantial. If the person is very angry. The person will feel defensible in telling someone what they are facing. If the person is expressively overwhelmed, attractive in an obsessive behavior suddenly appears like the keen thing to do.

- The badly-behaved is, acting on your feelings or needs in these instants perhaps works against your long-term goalmouths, the steady relations, upholding your self-confidence, and liberty from addictive behaviors.

Pieces of training

Levels of Training

The suitable amount of workout will be depending on your goalmouths and the wants of the customers or patients whom you are treating. The Levels of Exercise make it informal to plan the person DBT track. Four levels of training assist the development of your action knowledge and skill. The person can also check the calendar of proceedings to see our future in-person training opportunity our individual training plan should consider whether you want to:

Appropriate at Every Level

Level 1 – Outline to DBT: The person should Learn the rudimentary ethics of DBT, and they should decide if it is right for you and your customers **Level 2** – Therapy Fundamentals: Apply DBT rules and how DBT skills can assimilate into your already existing practice. You will also choose to offer DBT skills and training groups.

Level 3 – Complete Exercise in Standard DBT: Implement a full DBT program, founded on the innovative model developed and researched by a doctor.

Level 4 – Advanced DBT Training and Adaptations: Learn how to familiarize DBT for special inhabitants, e.g., children, teenagers

Ways to distract:

The person should do something, whatever to get your mind off your emotions. They should Play video games and straighten your closet, and they should get involved in some exercise.

They should always make sure that the action they choose doesn't strengthen your aching emotion. They should not play a violent video game when they are previously feeling annoyed. Instead, they should also visit their favorite coffee shop and get a mocha or whatsoever hot drink you love.

They should do enjoyable things for others: They can also support a friend, buy a homeless person a meal or helper. They should do very nice things for others not only takes your mind off your doubts for the instant but can also have the additional advantage of making sense of sense or purpose in your life.

They should read, watch, or listen to something that will bring on other emotions:

To do this, they should figure out what emotions they are feeling. Then they should read a book, watch a movie, or they can listen to their favorite music that suggests a feeling that is different than the one your sensation. When a person is feeling sad, they should listen to upbeat music. If you're annoyed, they should watch a funniness. When the person is feeling desperate, read about people who conserved in difficult times.

Thoughts:

This is one of the great to use when the person is in public, and they need a private way to sidetrack yourself. When the person Count 20 things they see around you that are blue, rerun the words in a poem in your head, you should count to 1000.

Engage your senses in something intense:

Let an ice cube dissolve in your hand, and they should take a hot bath or suck on a slice of lemon juice.

The importance of using DBT's distract skill:

The importance of using distraction is not to misuse it. The Sidetrack is a very real short-term solution that will also help you evade doing something you'll later regret, but it's not an answer to solving life's problems. In order to solve life's problems, they will have to attraction to other DBT services when you're in your astute mind.

Why distracting works:

The person should know Distracting works since it would help make a little interplanetary among you and whatever is hurtful you. An additional advantage is that occasionally off-putting also helps to change your painful emotions.

Skills

Interpersonal Effectiveness Module

The skills in this module are connected to networking with other people, particularly in difficult or possibly harmful circumstances. These skills are envisioned to help customer's purpose when trying to change something, create a request, or in trying to fight changes. The meaning is to aid the client in meeting their goalmouths in each state while evading any injury to the relationship or to the client's self-esteem.

Distress Tolerance Module

This module comprises skills that are tremendously significant yet frequently unnoticed: skills connecting to accepting, tolerating, and learning from suffering.

There are many other mental health treatment routines that emphasize on evading pain, changing difficult circumstances, or walking away from conditions that reason sorrow, but the suffering tolerance skills will learn through Dialectical Behavior Therapy emphasis on dealing with the pain and sorrow that is unavoidable to the human condition.

The suffering broad-mindedness module is divided into four disaster existence strategies. Self-soothing

They should focus on Improving the moment.
They should be thinking of the pros and cons.

In addition, there are many services that re-count to tolerant and standing the current situation, like fundamental receipt and readiness vs. willfulness.

Emotion Regulation Module

There are many clients who participate in DBT are struggling with personality or mood disorders and can advantage hugely from emotion rule skills.

Some of these skills that can help the person contract with their emotions include:
They should Be Classifying and labeling emotions.
They Are classifying obstacles to altering emotions.

And the Reducing vulnerability to "emotion mind.
They should attend Cumulative optimistic emotional events.

Snowballing mindfulness to present emotions.
Mindfulness Module

Booklovers of this blog are likely previously conscious of the many mindfulness-related services that can advantage them in their everyday life.

These skills include \What do I do to repetition essential mindfulness services?" like detecting, telling, and contributing. There are also "how" skills or skills will answer the question "How do I repetition core mindfulness services?", like non-judgment and working "One-mindfully" efficiently. Many of these mindfulness services feed into services from the other modules; for example, the nonjudgment invigorated in mindfulness is also stimulated in suffering broad-mindedness, and the detecting and telling skills can be obliging in classifying and classification emotions.

FAQs

Q. I really need to have hope to be in DBT?

Now .there are many people who come to DBT have very slight, if any, confidence that their suffering can be diminished. We also know that it is only with time that the person experiences with DBT will also help to upsurge hope. We ask that person "act conflicting" to their limited hope by presentation up frequently to meetings, working their skills, and letting the behavior to work!

Q. Is DBT a suicide anticipation treatment?

Not at all. Though most of the clients who come to DBT have long-lasting opinions about committing suicide and may have tried suicide on manifold occasions, the goal of DBT is not to stop suicide. The main goal is to help clients they want to build a life worth living by learning skills, tolerant who they are, and shifting what they can so that they will no longer need to kill themselves.

Q. Is DBT a basically trauma treatment?

Not at all. Most of the clients who come to DBT have sole or numerous shocks. Though, in DBT, we trust that if the person does not have the services to deal efficiently in their daily lives, they surely do not have the skills essential to work through trauma efficiently. As a result, trauma treatment is optional and shown after the client's complete skills exercise and are no longer showing self-harm and unhappy behaviors.

Q. Is DBT specifically only for those people with Borderline Character Disorder?

Not at all. While DBT was first shaped for persons with BPD that person chronically suicidal and hurting themselves, it is now used to treat persons with numerous identifies who have problems with sensitive dysregulation and distress tolerance also interpersonal associations, and impulsivity.

Q. I will be stimulated to talk about my past and childhood in DBT?

It depends. While early childhood experiences are helpful at the beginning of therapy to fully understand how the biosocial theory applies to you canceling/unsuccessful environment, biological indiscretions, DBT chiefly focuses on the present and future.

Q. Can DBT work for me?

Certainly! Most of the clients who come to DBT have had incomplete achievement in other therapies. This is typical because the other therapies did not efficiently treat the skills deficits that lead to their problems. DBT trusts that ahead "vision" into the details for difficult behaviors does not resolve the subject. Instead, they will be the first step altering the performances. However, vision is not unavoidably required to make changes.

Some of the Therapists told me that I'm not interested in getting better. Will I hear those things in DBT?

Not at all! In DBT we have the next opinions/molds about the person:

- The person is doing the best they can do.
- The person really wants to improve themselves.
- The person needs to do better, and they should try harder and be more interested in changing.
- The person may not have begun all their own problems, but they must resolve them anyway.
- The lives of unhappy, marginal persons are intolerable as they are currently being lived.

- The person must study new performances in all relevant contexts.

- The person cannot fail in therapy.

Q. How much fast does DBT work?

DBT is a marathon, not a dash. Varying performances takes time and tolerance. In some conditions, therapy is re-joining the associates in the brain by educating persons to perform, and they should think in different ways, which would lead to different outcomes. Being a DBT therapist, we do not imagine seeing major. If any changes throughout the first few months. It is typically right after the first few months of incessant action that clients start to see some changes.
Most of the adult DBT research proposes that it is not pending a separate has done with the prospectus two times that the real changes will take place. The research is done in the program also proposes that customers need 18 months in DBTSo the can also practice the most important change.

Q. Are there rules in DBT?

Only one. The DBT has a rule is that if you miss four successive individual sessions or four consecutive DBT skills collection meetings, you are cleared from the program. This is founded on the idea that DBT can only work if someone is coming to treatment. There are other rules for DBT treatment and for the Trinities DBT program; however, these are more flexible, and violations of them are learning opportunities.

Q. I've been kicked out of a lot of programs for the reason that of my problems. Will you also kick me out?

You will only kick out if nonappearance out. Any other subjects that come up defilements of guidelines, suicidal behavior, self-harm performance, intrusive treatment behaviors will be worked on with your counselor with the goalmouth of helping you not absenteeism out. Performances that happen in a group that are unhelpful or making the situation dangerous for other customers and the leaders may consequence in your not being allowable back in the group till a plan is created to stop the behaviors from frequent.
If that plan is in place without your missing four groups in a row, you will not be discharged.

Q. What is your policy on material use when in the program?

We need that the person should be willing to work on dipping and eventually stopping the use of illegal materials in order to be in the program. At the same time, contingent on the giving problems, material use may not be the top priority at the beginning of therapy unless it somehow causes and relates to behaviors like suicide and self-harm. When customers are done their first year of behavior, and they are still using substances. They would be necessary to approve to work on stopping the substance use if they are to endure in our program. This is for the reason that, in the additional year of action, clients will need to be livelier in discovering their own intelligent mind and adaptable their emotions, somewhat that is nearly unbearable when under the effect of substances.

Q. As I don't want to stop my self-harm, I'm able to come for DBT?

Most Probably, you should not because the DBT understands mutually unhappy and self-hurting actions as problem-solving strategies that, while possibly effective at the immediate to deal with suffering, will not assist you in the long-term. The performances also have many penalties that principal you to hurt more, and you will feel inferior.

When the person is not eager to work on substituting these plans with more real long-term plans, In all the DBT sessions would be filled with boundless fights for the reason that of contrary goals. Together you and the therapist would rapidly get burnt out. And the therapy would not be able to endure.

Q. Because my family members want me to go to DBT. and I'm not willing. And I'm not willing for this Should I come to DBT?

If you want to be in DBT treatment, it is improbable to work. Just showing up is not enough interest. You will be asked to repetition services and do homework outside of sessions, and if you do not have at smallest a little bit of motivation and interest in doing the work, changes are unlikely to occur.

Q. Let me know should I have to take DBT in my whole life?

No! DBT is a recovery-based model. This income that we will try our hardest to work with you on construction, a life that would not require you to be in DBT or any other treatment. Maximum customers who graduate from our program go on to live very meaningful lives with much-reduced suffering.

Q. What constitutes an absence in DBT?

They are not showing up to the meeting, stopping a session, or coming more than 15 minutes late to a session.

Q.It is true that the DBT has very severe attendance rules. What are they?

In DBT, if you miss four successive individual meetings or four successive DBT skills group sessions, you are cleared from the program. This is built on the idea that DBT will only work for you when you are coming for the treatment. There are no exempted nonappearances for things like being in the sanitorium and going on holiday, or being sick. Eventually, if a client misses a full month of treatment for any reason, the judgment and this is not right for them to be in DBT. In adding to the four-miss rule of standard DBT treatment, Trinities also has a piece of advice uttering that any more than six failures in ten months will probably lead to release. Coming late to meetings does not count as one of these failures for the reason that we want consumers to try and come to meetings even when they are running late.

Q. How can I be exempted from an absence? While there are comprehensible, defensible, and valid details for missing a session, there are no exempted absences in DPT.

Q. It is possible for me to make new friends in DPT

All those who are Clients who connect DBT will feel very calmed by how much they have shared with others in that program. While Connecting with others in DBT will also help the person practice their skills and feel reinforced

Though DBT will not allow the private relationships" with other consumers, the reason behind this means that secret-keeping is not allowable and that communications can be deliberated in individual sessions. These Clients are not allowable to talk about irresponsibility, If they are hurting and substance use with each other, also in a group or outdoor of the package.

Q. What if I don't like my assigned therapist? The person will be assigned a therapist also based upon who has an opening for the new customer.

So All memberships of the DBT team will also receive administration and conversation and are talented in providing you with the best DBT services. Then Smooth, if the person you do not feel like the allocated therapist is the best of them. We trust that the counselor can still help you study, repetition, and simplify services for the reason that we all effort in agreement with the same treatment model.

What if I'm not feeling comfortable and don't like the members of my skills group?

Typically, the clients will find at least one person in their skills group. Whom they are not feeling comfortable and feeling annoyed. We consider this as a great opportunity for you to learn how to not only tolerate being around people who you do not like but also repetition detecting your own bounds and have active relational connections.

Q. we can have a family and couple meetings? The Family and couples' sessions fundamentally are not usually a part of adult DBT treatment. Though, if the individual person and the therapist trust any of the next is happening, a family couple's session may ultimately be shown: The person will be asked for the next session meanwhile they want to discuss something with your family member important other and would like the separate therapist there as a trainer. There is a tragedy exploding in the Family that is receiving in the way of development family member significant other is doing something that is strengthening a behavior that you and the therapist are directing, and the counselor has faith in that you have not yet erudite the essential skills to achieve the situation on your own. There is a forthcoming risk to safety, and you have asked for your family noteworthy other to be communicated.

Q. I'm working person . will you accommodate my schedule?

We are having four DBT skills groups for customers to select to attend. Two of them are in the evenings, one is in the morning, and one is in the mid-afternoon. So once you choose a group that turns your schedule, the person will attend that group broadsheet for the distance of the program. Our individual counselors can typically accommodate your agenda, Monday through Friday, with schedules scheduled until 7 pm on some days.

Q. How much work is required from me outside of my sessions?

Individually week, you will be predictable to complete a homework task for the DBT skills group. This homework typically includes working skills and filling out a short questionnaire. The person will also complete a daily diary card that you bring together the DBT skills group and separate meetings. And the homework may also be allocated by your separate counselor if the person has confidence in it will be obliging in the attainment of your goals. While not obligatory, clients who appraisal what was taught in the skills group during the week and also incline to have more achievement in DBT.

Q. Can I stay in contact with my therapists outside the session?

Inappropriately, not. There are numerous reasons why those clients who join DBT at Trinities must take a break from any other therapists who would follow an exact construction and theory. If they have an outside therapist who has a dissimilar standpoint would be unclear for the client for the reason that the person may get very varied mails and proposals to know if a treatment is caring, This is one of the best to give the treatment a chance in its most pure form.

This is like a medicinal medic who will start with one research maintained medicine and add additional only when the first one is not sufficient on its own. Part of what makes DBT more real for customers is that there is frequent teamwork among skills trainers and distinct therapists. The level of vital collaboration would not be likely with a therapist who was not part of our side. Your current counselor may be amazing at assortment you with persuaded subjects, and you may choose to go back to them after applying for the program. Though, when you were sensation the attainment you were keen with your current therapist, you maybe would not be looking for a whole DBT program.

Q.When I'm enrolled in DBT, I can meet my counselor outside?

For the reason that any medical treatment is a careful ancillary treatment to DBT, you may keep sighted by your outside psychiatrist. Though, there are a few things to consider when doing so: DBT uses a technique called discussion to the client, which means that you will supervise discussing any subjects that come up with your psychiatrist. Your individual therapist will not be talking to the psychiatrist on your behalf under most circumstances if you have any talk therapy with your counselor. This is need to stop when you join our DBT program. Doings with your counselor are to emphasize only on subjects connected to medicine and medical circumstances.

You regularly Asked Questions About Trinities Adult DBT

Q. Do you take insurance?

At the present time, we are taking most insurances, Medicare and Medic also.

Q. Are there other services that I can be part of while I wait for my DBT screening?

This is possible because when you will join any of the services on the Adult Outpatient Unit while you will be for your broadcast. There are some medicine management services and group therapy, and also short-term individual therapy. The person will need to go through the consumption to partake in these services. Feel free to let the intake clinician know that you are on the waitlist for DBT.

Q. Is your program co-ed BDT?

We have together male and female customers, and also we have male and female therapists in our program.

Q. When I complete the task, what will happen? When the person has done the one and two years or has comprehensible with your discrete therapist that you have reached your DBT goals, you will become alumna from our DBT program. Many customers continue to seek separate therapy from breadwinners outside the program, join peer-run provision sets, or seam other therapeutic collections on the Adult Outpatient Unit at Trinities.

Others would not continue with any formal therapy and get provisions from their atmosphere only. Linehan, who had writhed with these issues when she was younger, though that modifying traditional CBT might help. One very important addition was validation – interactive that there was a cause people touched the way they did and observed for the in-force shards of their responses. The receipt was an additional dangerous change. We will also tell the people that we admit to them where they are in the way they are. There is a cause of people to respond the way they do. In the same opinion, she presented the idea of dialectics. Tension is a state. Where the person has two things that appear to be contraries, and yet can together be true at the same time. The main tension in working with DBT is this.when the person is there is a reason where they are, and assumed what you'd been done, and it will make sense that you counter the way you do. What you’re doing right now isn’t working for you. So there is a need to change what you’re doing.

Conclusion

DBT helps individuals indulge in useful activities and practice different skills to help individuals deal with their problems more effectively. Though many skills are incorporated in the individual through the treatment, emotional regulation, and distress tolerance can be given special importance as the success rate of the treatment depends on the effectiveness of both these skills.

CPSIA information can be obtained
at www.ICGtesting.com
Printed in the USA
BVHW091339210621
610125BV00005B/1280

9 781892 504166